Great Teacher Projects

Great Teacher Projects

Laura Mayne

Illustrations by Scot Ritchie

The BOSTON
MILLS PRESS

A Boston Mills Press Book

Library and Archives Canada Cataloguing in Publication

Mayne, Laura, 1957-
    Great teacher projects / Laura Mayne ;
illustrations by Scot Ritchie.

Includes bibliographical references and index.
ISBN-13: 978-1-55046-524-2 (bound).
ISBN-10: 1-55046-524-4 (bound)
ISBN-13: 978-1-55046-510-5 (pbk.)
ISBN-10: 1-55046-510-4 (pbk.)

1. Creative activities and seat work. 2. Activity
programs in education. I. Ritchie, Scot II. Title.

LB1027.25.M29 2009   371.3   C2009-902142-0

Publisher Cataloging-in-Publication Data (U.S.)

Mayne, Laura.
    Great teacher projects : K–8 / Laura Mayne ;
Scot Ritchie.
[160] p. : col. ill. ; cm.
Includes bibliographical references and index.
Summary: Teacher-tested and approved projects
for use in Grade K-8 classrooms. Covers many
subjects and curriculum areas; tips include book
tie-ins for recommended classroom reading,
modifying projects for different ages and abilities.
ISBN-13: 978-1-55046-524-2 (bound)
ISBN-10: 1-55046-524-4 (bound)
ISBN-13: 978-1-55046-510-5 (pbk.)
ISBN-10: 1-55046-510-4 (pbk.)
1. Education, Primary—Activity programs.
I. Ritchie, Scot. II. Title.
372.5 dc22   LB1537.M39   2009

Published in 2009 by Boston Mills Press
132 Main Street,
Erin, Ontario N0B 1T0
Tel 519-833-2407
Fax 519-833-2195

In Canada
Distributed by Firefly Books Ltd.
66 Leek Crescent
Richmond Hill, Ontario L4B 1H1

In the United States
Distributed by Firefly Books (U.S.) Inc.
P.O. Box 1338, Ellicott Station
Buffalo, New York 14205

www.bostonmillspress.com

Editor: Kathleen Fraser
Design: PageWave Graphics Inc.

Printed in China

The publisher gratefully acknowledges the financial support for our publishing program by the Government
of Canada through the Book Publishing Industry Development Program.

"Tashkent" in *Some of the Kinder Planets*. Copyright © 1993 by Tim Wynne-Jones. First published in
Canada by Groundwood Books Ltd. Reprinted by kind permission of the publisher.

To my parents,
Matthew and Bruna Gumieniak,
my first teachers

This book has been designed to be user-friendly. You'll see that there are three tables of contents: the first is alphabetical, in the order the projects appear in the book. The second is by subject. You'll notice that many projects cover more than one subject area. The third is by grade level, though most of the projects can be adapted up or down.

There are also several lists of kinds of projects throughout the book to facilitate finding the right project for the right time, as well as lots of "teacher tips" along the way. Teacher tips are set in italics in the contents.

Each project begins with an "at-a-glance" summary followed by information on Grades, Subjects, Time Frame and Materials.

Contents

*See over for a table
of contents of projects
by subject.*

Projects by Subject

Library Skills

Math

Media Studies

Music

Phys. Ed.

Science

Social Studies

Team Building / Character Education

Teacher Tips

In consulting this list of Projects by Subject, you will notice that many of the projects are suggested for more than one subject. Most of the projects in this book are meant to be cross-curricular — crossing subjects and methods of learning and instruction. Most are also able to be used and adapted for most grade levels from K to 8; however, for suggested Projects by Grade Level, see pages 12–13.

See over for a table of contents of projects by grade level.

Projects by Grade Level

Most of the projects in this book can be adapted for use with most grade and ability levels, but some are especially suited to a particular range of grades. Here's an outline of suggested grade levels.

Great for Grades K-2

Great for Grades 3-6

Great for Grades 5-8

A Note on Grade Level

Most of the projects in this book can be modified up or down to meet the grade and ability levels of your students. To keep things consistent, you will see the following terms used to designate grade level groupings:

Younger grades refers to grade levels K to 3.

Middle grades refers to grade levels 4 to 6

Upper grades refers to grade levels 7 and 8.

The diversity of students in our classrooms requires us to modify and accommodate for Special Needs students, learners of English as a Second Language, students with an IEP, or other students who require special consideration. Teachers must work within the guidelines of their school board or district as well as applying knowledge about the child's learning style and a little imagination. Through thoughtful consideration of all these factors, you will be able to meet the needs of all the students in your care.

Acknowledgments

Heartfelt thanks to Kathy Fraser, friend and editor. It has been an A+ experience working with you on this project.

Special thanks to John Denison at Boston Mills Press who had the original idea for this book, and to Noel Hudson for his input.

Thank you so much:

- to the people at Firefly Books

- to Scot Ritchie for the cheerful illustrations. It's as if you were right there in the classroom!

- to Andrew Smith and Joseph Gisini at PageWave Graphics for a great design

- to all the great teachers who contributed projects, including the shy ones who wished to contribute anonymously

- to Bill McNamara and Ed Pernu, with fond memories

- to James Parkinson from Anne Bancroft and Dorothy Gale

To Betty Borowski, my teaching partner, motherhood guru, common sense touchstone, and Lucy to my Ethel (or is it the other way around?), thank you for years of teaching and life adventures.

To Mary Fraser, Laura Fraser, Jennifer Gumieniak, Fatima Wittemund, and Dallas Borris, the young new teachers in my life—now it's your turn!

To all my students over the years, especially the Junior and Senior Kindergarten students 2003–2008 at St. Francis of Assisi School, Mississauga, Ontario. Teaching you was the greatest job in the world. I was guaranteed to laugh every single day!

To my family, Moo, Mary and Brian, Tom, Rob and Liza, Jennifer, Matthew and Erin, thanks for listening to 27 years worth of teaching stories.

To Gerard and Maddy, thank you and love you!

Introduction

FREE KNOWLEDGE
Available Monday to Friday
Bring your own container!

This saying from some long-forgotten source has hung on the wall in my classroom for the past 27 years. It's an exciting concept, free knowledge. Our students get it from us and we get it from them. It's everywhere, especially in this technological age. It's addictive!

On any curriculum document you'll see a lengthy list of specific expectations that teachers must provide when delivering programs: flexibility, challenge, integration, reflective practice, differentiated instruction, relevance, balance and more.

What all teachers want and need are classroom projects that actually motivate students and make the light bulb above their heads click on while fulfilling these government, district and school requirements.

The great projects in this book have been chosen from among the favorites of great teachers who submitted their tried-and-true, classroom-tested projects to share with their colleagues everywhere. Without breaking the budget or requiring complicated equipment and materials, each of these projects contributes in some way to a successful and enjoyable whole-year class experience.

Some of these are great projects in the traditional sense: *vavagaga* (teacher lingo for "visually appealing and gorgeously aesthetic") has its place, for sure. On the other hand, some of the projects are "great" not by that measure, but by their value as group-building exercises. Some are simple and yet effective, some serve to scaffold knowledge, some create cultural literacy and general knowledge, and some are just plain fun.

If there's one thing a teacher loves, it's an idea that really works in the classroom. These ideas fit the bill, hit the mark, and bring learning to life!

Alphabet Adventure

There are 26 letters in the alphabet, and 26,000 ways to use them. Here are a few.

Grades K–8

Subjects Language Arts

Time Frame Will vary depending on the project

Materials Paper, pencils, imagination

For younger students

- Do a shared writing chart. Pick a category and try to come up with one word for each letter of the alphabet (for example, animals, food, names, toys).
- Sing fun alphabet songs. Some favorites are:

  Backwards ABCs (to the same tune as the traditional ABC song)

  Write the letters from Z to A on the board or on a chart, and point to each one as you sing. End with "now we know our Z Y Xs, next time we will go to Texas."

  I Am Learning (to the tune of London Bridge)

  I am learning letter A
  Letter A, letter A
  I am learning letter A
  a a a a a (for this line sing the sound the letter makes, not its name)

In the middle grades

- Give one page of a newspaper to each student or pair of students. Each student should have a highlighter. Each individual or team highlights one word that starts with each letter of the alphabet on their newspaper page. This can also be done as a race.

- Challenge students to write sentences that feature words in alphabetical order, for example, "Michael never ordered pancakes." Students may pick their starting letter and work at writing longer and longer sentences.

In the upper grades

- Have students research the history of the English alphabet. Students can make a large chart showing various alphabets from around the world (Greek, Cyrillic, Egyptian, Arabic, etc.) and use it to compare and contrast the features of each one.

- Students will write an autobiography in which each paragraph features a reflection on a facet of the student's life that begins with a given letter, for example, H for hobbies, F for family. Depending on the grade and ability level, students may be required to use all the letters or only a given number.

Book Tie-ins

There are thousands of alphabet books, from simple ABCs to wildly creative volumes. Here are some favorites:

So Many Bunnies by Rick Walton

A to Zen by Ruth Wells

Antics by Cathi Hepworth

Arlene Alda's ABC by Arlene Alda

Q is for Duck by Mary Elting and Michael Folsom

Tomorrow's Alphabet by George Shannon

Agenda Day

Adopt Agenda Day in your classroom once a month, every two weeks or every week. Let your students choose the order in which the activities of their day will unfold. Students enjoy the freedom to choose their own timetable, look forward to a change from the regular routine, and develop time-management skills by taking part in Agenda Day.

How you structure your day and offer choices to your students will depend on the grade level of the class.

For younger students, Agenda Day can be as simple as allowing them to vote on which subject they would like to do first, for instance, Math or Language Arts.

In the middle grades, the assignments for the morning or afternoon can be written on the board and students may choose the order in which they would like to do them. You could announce the times at which you expect the students to change to another subject.

In upper grades, the reading and assignments for the half or full day can be posted on the board and each student can choose his or her own timetable.

Middle and upper grade students still need to be guided, so use the gradual release-of-responsibility model by starting off with a shorter time period before jumping to a half- or full-day Agenda Day.

Students who have difficulties with time management can be monitored or given a checklist, and required to check in with you at specific intervals.

Book Tie-ins
Would You Rather...
by John Burningham

Amaryllis Plant

Students observe the stages of growth of an amaryllis plant.

Grades K–4

Subjects Science, Language Arts, Art, Math

Time Frame Several weeks. Winter is best because that is when amaryllis bulbs are widely available.

Materials An amaryllis plant in the early stages of growth; a ruler, chart paper

An amaryllis *(hippeastrum)* plant is especially suited to this project as it grows very quickly and has a strong stem that can withstand enthusiastic measuring by young students. You can purchase one at grocery store or florist. Bring the plant into the classroom when it is in the early growth stages but not yet blooming (approximately 6 inches / 15 cm tall).

The beginning of this project is a good opportunity for vocabulary development. Discuss the parts of a plant, care of plants (research the care required for this specific plant on the computer), and make charts and or diagrams using your findings.

Have the students choose the best place in the classroom for the plant to be located, based on the factors discussed. Make a schedule for watering and measuring so each child is involved.

Measure the plant each day. Use the daily measurements for mathematical calculations: students can figure out how many inches or centimeters the plant grows each day and week, average growth, total growth, and other addition and subtraction questions based on growth.

Keep a log to note daily growth numbers, to say whose turn it is to measure the plant and water the plant, to create a list of words that describe the growing plant, and to compare the size of the plant to common classroom objects (taller, shorter, same), and more. Students can draw the plant in various stages of growth and write accompanying details.

For younger students, a chart-paper observation log can be a shared writing activity, with children taking turns with the pen. The teacher can put help put together a digital photo display.

In the middle and upper grades, students can keep individual logs, documenting a detailed description of the plant as well as the particulars of its growth. Students can work in groups on a digital photo display.

Other activities could include brainstorming a list of all the flowers the children can think of, or trying to make an A–Z chart with a flower name for each letter.

Book Tie-ins

Allison's Zinnia by Anita Lobel
Flower Fairies Alphabet by Cecily Mary Barker
The Flower Alphabet Book by Jerry Pallotta
The Sunflower Parable by Liz Curtis Higgs
This Is the Sunflower by Lola M. Schaefer

Art Project

In this project, students will research the life and work of an artist and recreate one of that artist's works.

Grades 1–8

Subjects Art, Language Arts, Library Skills

Materials A selection of books on art and artists from your school or public library; a variety of pictures of famous works of art; a supply of art materials such as paper, oil pastels, paint, charcoal pencils

This project can be done successfully with many different grade levels by modifying the expectations for the written project and finished product. It is one of the all-time most successful projects in our school, and most requested by teachers working with our teacher-librarian.

Brainstorm with the class the names of famous artists, paintings, sculptures and works of art that they have heard of. Use a flow chart or mind map to record these on chart paper. (Students will refer to it again at the end of the project.)

On another day, do a book talk for the class with art books. Allow students to share and discuss the books over several days.

Show and display postcards or photos of selected paintings. Use postcards from art galleries, color photocopies from books, or downloaded pictures from websites. Arrange to have five or six more pictures than you have students so that each student will have a choice of several works and no one will be stuck with the last one. (Depending on the grade level, choose works of art that students will later be able to reproduce without frustration.) Have a group sharing session where students share their observations and feelings about the art.

After several days observing the art, students will choose from the display a work of art that appeals to him/her. Students will then work individually to write in their journals their thoughts and feelings about that work, including how they feel while looking at it, anything they might already know about the work or the artist, what shapes and colors they see, and some words to describe the work. This journal work could later be edited, rewritten and added to the written component of the project.

The assignment is in two parts. Students will reproduce the work of art after consulting with the teacher about medium, size and method. A hint for students when reproducing the picture is to cover the picture with clear plastic wrap or a plastic sheet and divide it into quadrants with a permanent marker. This helps them focus on each section of the work.

Students will also research the artist following the criteria/rubric established by the teacher: include country of origin, style of art, personal facts about the artist, etc. The length and format of the research project will vary depending on grade level. *Younger students* could limit their research to the

name of the artist, the country he/she came from, and a couple of facts. *Upper-grade students* can format their information into a PowerPoint presentation.

Work together with your teacher-librarian to teach appropriate research skills, how to take notes, and how to format the information. See *Research Projects* at page 43 for more ideas.

When the art works are complete, each student will present his or her work of art to the class along with a short summary of their research about the artist. The art should be displayed in the school, each work alongside the picture of the original. Caption the display "The New Masters." Invite other classes, school administration and perhaps parents in to view them.

A visit to a local art gallery is a good tie-in to this project. On a visit to a major art gallery following completion of this project with a class, gallery staff were impressed with the level of knowledge the students displayed while looking at the art. Both gallery and school staff were delighted when one student bounded up to a painting, calling, "Look, it's my Picasso!"

Or you and your class can watch videos/DVDs on artists. Good choices include *Linnea in Monet's Garden* (available from Icarus Films with educational rights); *Auryn's Painted Tales* series (available from Microcinema International www.microcinemadvd.com with educational rights); and the *Painting Pictures* series (available from Sound Venture productions www.soundventure.com/onlinestore with educational rights — this series is geared to young children, but is equally interesting to older children).

A related project for *upper-grade students* is to follow the same format, but instead of a work of art and artist, have each student research a famous building and architect.

Book Tie-ins

Getting to Know the World's Greatest Artists series by Mike Venezia

Smart About Art series (various authors)

Linnea in Monet's Garden by Christina Bjork and Lena Anderson

I Spy, An Alphabet in Art by Lucy Micklethwait

Lulu and the Flying Babies by Posy Simmonds

Birds

Decorate your classroom with lifelike, life-size, student-made drawings of birds. Students learn careful observation, use of fine detail and symmetry.

Grades 3–8

Subjects Science, Art, Language Arts

Time Frame Two or three lessons

Materials Thick white or cream-colored paper or Bristol board, markers and or colored pencils, photos of birds, scissors

Gather close-up, whole-body photos of various types of birds (check nature magazines, download from internet). Show the pictures to the class and discuss characteristics of birds, such as body shape and parts, and specialized features such as wings and beaks, etc.

Have each student choose a photo. Students will find out the typical height and size of the bird, and sketch a life-size outline of the body on a piece of thick manila paper or Bristol Board. After the sketch is done, cut out the paper, and first sketch (lightly in pencil) then color the features of the individual bird. Complete the other side as well.

A short, written research project about the chosen bird could also be completed by each student by hand or on computer.

Book Tie-ins

Have You Seen Birds?
by Joanne Oppenheim, illustrated
in Plasticine art by Barbara Reid

Field Guides to Birds by National
Geographic, National Audubon Society,
Smithsonian

Bird DK Eyewitness Book

How to Paint the Portrait of a Bird by
Jacques Prevert

The Birds in My Life
by The Supreme Master Ching Hai

Display ideas:
- Hang the birds with fishing wire from the classroom ceiling (check local health and safety regulations first).
- Make a giant tree out of brown construction paper on a bulletin board and perch the birds on it.
- Use a wire hanger, cover the opening with paper, write the name of the bird on the paper and hang the bird from the bottom.
- Get small branches from the ground in the schoolyard, student's yards or other local places, and perch the birds on the branches on a bulletin board OR use an adhesive tack product to attach the birds to the branches so it appears that the bird has landed on the branch.

Alternative presentations:
- Use a Bristol Board card (like a baseball card, only larger) for each type of bird. (Decide on a standard format students will follow.)
- Make a shape book. Trace the original outline of the bird on plain paper and write facts about the bird by category on each page.

Book Report in a Bag

Teachers are always looking for ways to freshen up the traditional book report. Here is one that students enjoy.

Grades 4–8

Subjects Language Arts, Art, Math

Time Frame One to two weeks or longer

Materials White paper bag with handles for each student; construction paper for work cards

Students choose a book to read and report on.

Middle grade students could read a short chapter book. Be sure to have a selection of books at various reading levels, and to have more books than you have students.

In upper grades, have students choose from a set of books preselected by the teacher, or allow them to choose their own. You could further refine the project by having all students choose a certain genre (for example, science fiction), or have groups of five to six students each working on one genre. Following their individual work, the students who worked on each genre could put together a presentation for the class outlining features of the genre as well as a brief bibliography of the books they read.

Give each student a white paper bag with handles (approximately 8 by 10 inches / 20 by 25 cm or slightly smaller). On one side of the bag students will draw a cover for their book. On the other side they will create a collage featuring various aspects of the book.

Have students measure and cut out of construction paper a number of 5-by-5-inch / 13 x 13 cm cards. (This is the Math component of the project.) On these cards they will summarize various elements of the book. You will determine the number of cards according to the grade and ability level of the students. Basic topics for cards can include the following:

1. Theme
2. Plot
3. Three Major Characters: for each character, students write the character's names, three words to describe their personality, three words to describe their physical appearance
4. Favorite Character
5. Book Facts: author, number of pages, genre, publisher, year of publication
6. Problem / Resolution

The cards will then be placed into the decorated bag. Students will also include a handmade artifact related to the book in their bags. For example, a student who read *Charlie and the Chocolate Factory* created a homemade chocolate bar; another student who read *Underground to Canada* linked florist wire loops together to make a chain, representing the shackles worn by slaves. Once all the material has been created, the book report in a bag is handed in to the teacher.

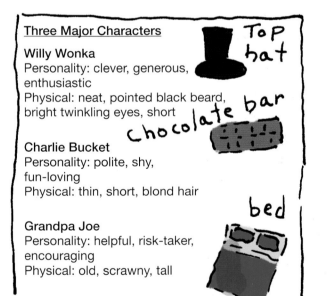

Three Major Characters

Willy Wonka
Personality: clever, generous, enthusiastic
Physical: neat, pointed black beard, bright twinkling eyes, short

Top hat

chocolate bar

Charlie Bucket
Personality: polite, shy, fun-loving
Physical: thin, short, blond hair

Grandpa Joe
Personality: helpful, risk-taker, encouraging
Physical: old, scrawny, tall

bed

For upper grades, students can also complete a response journal entry about the book or use graphic organizers to summarize an aspect of the book. Or you can devise any other activity that suits your students, including giving them a free choice for one of the cards.

Book Tie-ins

Creative Book Reports: Fun Projects with Rubrics for Fiction and Nonfiction by Jane Feber

Book Talk on Video

This project gives students a chance to work both in front of and behind the camera to write and deliver a compelling book talk.

Grades K–8

Subjects Language Arts, Drama, Media

Time Frame Several weeks

Materials Selection of novels or picture books; video camera

This project gives students a chance to study and emulate appropriate on-air skills such as speaking slowly and clearly, using good posture, projecting personality, and being prepared. These skills are important for many other types of presentations. Students also enjoy the teamwork and the process of making and especially watching the video.

Work with your teacher-librarian to make the book selections. Make sure you have more books than students so no one will feel as if theirs was the last choice.

Book Tie-ins

DK Readers: Jobs People Do — A Day in the Life of a TV Reporter
by Linda Hayward

TV Reporters (Community Helpers)
by Tracey Boraas

How Do I Become a TV Reporter?
by Mindi Englart

Reading Rainbow DVDs are available from GPN Educational Media: www.shopgpn.com

In upper grades, students can read a novel or a picture book and talk about the book on video using a prearranged format. *In the younger grades,* children can be filmed retelling a story that has been read to them.

Or, *to combine activities for different grade levels,* have students from upper grades help prepare and film their younger reading buddies' book talks.

As a class, watch a video or DVD of a program such as *Reading Rainbow* in which students do a brief book talk. Determine a format for the video presentation that will be used by the students. Post it on a chart in the classroom and, *in upper grades,* provide a copy on paper to each student including a rubric explaining how their work will be assessed.

Do a book talk with the class to introduce them to the books you have brought in to the classroom. Make sure the books you choose cover a wide range of topics. Give students access to the books. Encourage them to explore many before choosing one. Have each student choose a book that appeals to him or her.

As students read, they can make notes that will help them put together a presentation that follows the format you have already determined. Students read the book, then conference with the teacher, prepare and write their presentation, record it on video and save.

A simple backdrop can be created in the classroom, or a school setting can be the backdrop for the on-camera reports. Depending on the grade level, students may be used to operate the camera and as directors, prompters, etc. The finished video or DVD (edited by teacher or students) can be circulated among families one night at a time for viewing.

When former students come back for a visit or run into you at the mall, it's always interesting to hear them reminisce about the things they remember and enjoyed most about their time in your class. Many students have spoken of the making and watching of these book talks as one project that was an especially fun time and a good memory.

Books for Younger Students

Students in upper grades relax and experience positive feedback when reading and writing for the youngest students in the school.

Grades 3–8

Subjects Language Arts, Art, possibly Science, Social Studies, Math

Time Frame A couple of weeks

Materials The usual supplies for publishing student books

In this project, your older students will write books for younger students.

You may already know a variation on this project, where older students become "reading buddies" with younger students, and help them learn to read. Some teachers look at tried-and-true projects and think to themselves "Oh, this again." But there's a reason why we come back to them year after year. They're solid. They work. The trick is in adding freshness each time, in tailoring the project to your class, and in recognizing that though it's not your first experience with it, it is new to your students.

This is also a great project for English language learners or older students still at an emergent writing level. Another benefit that comes from older students writing for younger ones is fostering a spirit of community within the school. Young children love it when they recognize their reading buddies in the halls or schoolyard.

Choose the grade level at which your students' books will be targeted. Determine with the teacher of the younger grade what type of books would be appropriate — for example, simple story books, retelling classic stories, nonfiction books that tie into curriculum unit themes. (Science and Social Studies would be especially appropriate.)

Possible books your students can create:
- alphabet book, perhaps on a theme
- fairy tales reduced to simple sentences and pictures
- joke book
- predictable book (with repeated lines)
- a personal experience story
- animal fact book

Begin by sharing with your class some books aimed at the grade level they will be writing for. A quick consultation with the teacher of the younger grade or your teacher-librarian will give you a starting point. Before reading the books aloud to the class, tell them they will be writing their own book to share with younger students, so they should be looking at features such as vocabulary, style and format.

As a class, do a lesson or two on those features so that students have a clear picture of what their target writing level is.

This project can be done in groups or by individuals. After writing and editing a rough copy, students will write and illustrate a good copy. This can be done on computer or by hand.

Choose a day for sharing the books. A good logistical tip is to spread the students out between the two classrooms to avoid overcrowding. Make a plan beforehand with the other class's teacher for pairing up the children so that not a lot of time is spent organizing.

Also, prepare the older students by giving some guidelines for sharing with younger students: for example, read slowly and clearly, give them time to look at the pictures, ask them questions about what you are reading etc.

The sharing time could end with a treat for both classes such as cookies or lollipops.

Book Tie-ins

Young Author's Day at Pokeweed Public School by John Bianchi

Brown Paper Characters

This project produces large 3D models that make a great classroom or school library displays.

Grades 4–8

Subjects Any

Time Frame One or two planning/instructional sessions, several sessions for painting and stuffing

Materials A roll of brown kraft paper, paint in different colors, newspaper for stuffing

Decide on the desired size for the finished product and cut a length of brown paper twice that size. Fold it in the middle. The front and back will be painted and then stapled together and stuffed with newspaper to create a large, 3D model.

In pencil, sketch in an outline of the person or figure the students want to represent on the front and back of the brown paper. When the outline is finished, paint in the outline plus any details. When the front is dry, paint the back as well.

After the back is dry, cut the figure to the desired shape and staple around three sides, leaving one of the long sides open. Carefully stuff wadded up newspaper inside, making sure the stuffing is equally distributed. Staple up the remaining side and display.

This project works well for a variety of topics such as:

- study of ancient Egypt (Egyptian characters)
- native studies (totem poles)
- novel studies (characters from the novel)
- medieval studies (characters in period dress)

Or students can make likenesses of themselves by tracing their body and following the same format for stapling and stuffing. Paint a face and hair, and dress in the student's actual clothing. This is a great project for parent interview time. When the parents enter the classroom, there appears to be someone sitting at each desk! Parents can take their brown paper son or daughter home after the interview.

Book Tie-ins

Brown Paper Teddy Bear by Catherine Allison

What Can You Do With a Paper Bag? by Judith Cressy

Look What You Can Make With Paper Bags by Judy Burke

Butterfly Life Cycle in Pasta

A fun and memorable project in which students learn about the life cycle of a butterfly and represent each stage with a different type of pasta.

Grades K–3

Subjects Science, Art, Language Arts, Music

Time Frame One to two lessons

Materials Books and charts about the life cycle of a butterfly; green Bristol board; glue; pasta shapes:

  acini de pepe (dots) represents egg stage

  fusilli (corkscrews) represents
    caterpillar stage

  conchiglie (shells) represents
    chrysalis stage

  farfalle (bow ties) represents
    butterfly stage

Discuss the life cycle of a butterfly using books, charts and DVDs as visual aids. Make a class chart showing the four stages of the life cycle.

Depending on the grade level, provide students with a large leaf cutout made of green Bristol board, or have them trace a template and cut out. In the four corners of the leaf, have students glue down several pieces of the appropriate pasta to symbolize the stages of growth of a butterfly, starting with the egg stage at the top.

Students can label the display according to their skills. *Junior Kindergarten* students could cut out and glue labels; *Senior Kindergarten* students could label each stage. *Older students* could add a sentence or two describing each stage of development.

Students could also write and illustrate journal entries, in both fiction and non-fiction formats, about butterflies.

Book Tie-ins

From Caterpillar to Butterfly (Let's Read and Find Out series, Stage One) by Deborah Heiligman and Bari Weissman

Are You a Butterfly? by Judy Allen and Tudor Humphries

Where Butterflies Grow by Joanne Ryder and Lynne Cherry

Eyewitness: Butterfly and Moth by Paul Whalley

DK Readers: Born to be a Butterfly by DK Publishing

The Very Hungry Caterpillar by Eric Carle

Dover Publications has a small and very inexpensive book called *Little Butterflies Stained Glass Coloring Book*. Children enjoy coloring the butterflies and taking the pages home to mount on a window. Another Dover publication is *Fun With Butterflies Stencil Book*. The stencils from this book are fun for the children to use in an art center.

Little kids love to sing. If you can play three chords on a guitar they will think you are a rock star! Look online for songs that fit your curriculum and are sung to familiar tunes. These are fun songs to accompany this project.

The Life of a Butterfly
(to the tune of *"Skip To My Lou"*)

I'm a caterpillar, wiggle with me,
I'm a caterpillar, wiggle with me,
I'm a caterpillar, wiggle with me,
What'll I be, my darlin'?

A chrysalis, now sleep like me,
A chrysalis, now sleep like me,
A chrysalis, now sleep like me,
What'll I be, my darlin'?

A butterfly, come fly with me,
A butterfly, come fly with me,
A butterfly, come fly with me,
What'll I be, my darlin'?

Now all together, let's do all three.
A caterpillar, a chrysalis,
A butterfly — three.
Move your body like this with me.
The life of a butterfly, darlin'.

I'm a Butterfly
(to the tune of *"Frère Jacques"*)

I'm an egg. I'm an egg
On a little leaf, on a little leaf.
Soon I'll be a caterpillar.
Soon I'll be a caterpillar.
Watch me eat! Watch me eat!

I'm a caterpillar. I'm a caterpillar
You're one too, you're one too.
Soon we'll both be butterflies.
Soon we'll both be butterflies.
Something new! Something new!

I'm a chrysalis. I'm a chrysalis
Warm and dry, warm and dry.
Changing from the inside
Changing from the inside
Into a butterfly! Into a butterfly!

I'm a butterfly. I'm a butterfly
Flying all around, flying all around.
Looking for a flower
Looking for a flower
Searching up and down.
Searching up and down.

(both songs from www.mrsjonesroom.com)

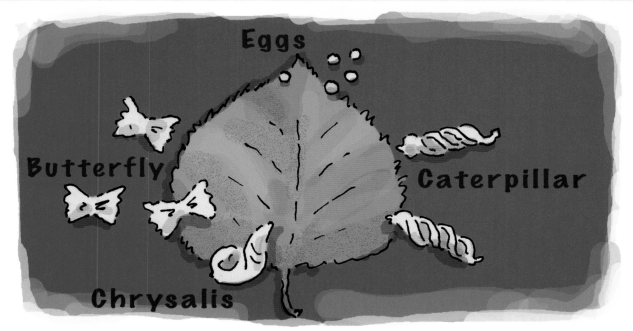

35

Choral Reading

Kids have more fun reading out loud when they speak together in a group.

Grades K–8

Subjects Language Arts, Drama

Time Frame One to two lessons to introduce the concept of choral reading and teach strategies, several lessons for group practice, several lessons for performances and follow-up

Materials Copies of the choral reading selection for each group member. Choose one or more readings.

Choral reading (or speaking, if the material is memorized) is an interpretive reading in unison by a group. By reading in a group, students can practice oral reading skills without the anxiety that some children feel about reading aloud in front of a group.

This is a fun way to build communication skills. Students are continually assessed by methods requiring a high level of skill in communicating information: for example, in presentations, debates, conferences and oral retells. Working in a choral reading group builds skill levels and confidence in the areas of teamwork, group accountability and interdependence, all of which are valuable tools for many learning areas.

Do a whole class lesson to teach the children about various ways to use their voices. Strategies include:
- loud and soft voices
- high and low voices
- slow and fast words or lines
- body movement
- sound effects such as snapping fingers, whooshing for wind, etc.
- using one voice, part of the group or the whole group together for various parts of the reading

Give each group copies of their choral reading selection, one for each member of the group. You can have the whole class working on the same selection (a good way to begin) or divide the class into groups, each working on a different reading (better for experienced

choral readers). Direct each group to meet in a different part of the room, read through the selection, and begin discussing and practicing.

Circulate among the groups listening, observing the dynamics and making anecdotal notes about students who are displaying leadership, those who are working well in this cooperative setting, those who are very quiet or displaying behavior that is a problem for the group, etc.

When groups have had sufficient time to prepare, each group will perform their choral reading piece for the class. The students who act as the audience should be prepared to offer specific feedback about the performance, such as noting how the group made their presentation effective and how each group's presentation differed from the others.

For younger students who are nonreaders or early readers, choose a short selection that can be easily memorized by frequent repetition. Post the selection on chart paper with illustrations that provide visual cues.

Book Tie-ins

Crackers and Crumbs: Chants for Whole Language by Sonja Dunn and Lou Pamenter

All Together Now: 200 of Sonja Dunn's Best Chants by Sonja Dunn

Circles

A creative and fun art lesson. Your students will surprise you!

Large

Grades K–8

Subjects Art

Time Frame One lesson to fill in the circles, one lesson to compare and discuss what they drew

Materials White paper with square border and circle (roughly 7-inch square, 5-inch diameter circle / 17 cm square, 12 cm diameter circle), crayons, colored pencils, markers

Draw a large circle on the board. Get a few suggestions from students about what they imagine the circle to be (but not too many ideas, as you want students to use their imaginations without too much influence from the discussion). Talk about the wide variety of things the circle could represent or be turned into.

Give the students a sheet of paper with a square border and a circle inside. Students draw something using the circle, cut around the border and arrange the squares in a rectangle shape on a bulletin board to make a quilt-like display with the results.

Discourage students from using the examples discussed in the classroom or sharing ideas with friends. You want as many unique ideas as possible. Permit each student two or three tries, then student or teacher may choose one for the finished product.

Small

Grades K–8

Subjects Art

Time Frame One lesson

Materials White paper with square border and 16 small circles (roughly 5 inches / 12 cm square border divided into 16 small squares, in each small square a circle roughly ¾ inch / 2 cm diameter), crayons, colored pencils, markers

Use this as an alternate or additional circle project; the smaller circles will inspire different ideas.

Give students a page with 16 small circles, and ask them to add to them to make pictures of things. When finished, share as a class. Discuss categories (perhaps make a list or chart), most creative ideas, most commonly drawn etc.

For younger students, reduce the number of circles to three or four. *In middle grades,* give students eight circles to fill in.

The variety of student responses from these exercises lends itself to discussion of:
- ways in which each individual is unique
- the diverse responses of any given group of people, even when given identical instructions
  - the nature and development of creativity
  - the theory of multiple intelligences (see page 77)

Technology

Depending on your school, you may have access to a shiny new computer lab, one ancient computer in your classroom, or no computers at all. School boards and districts each have their own policies and curriculum regarding use of computers in the classroom. The projects in this book do not assume widespread computer access in the school. If you are fortunate enough to have it, most of the projects can be adapted to include the use of computers.

Many schools have paint programs, reading programs, word processing programs, spreadsheets and other specialized software such as PowerPoint, KidPix and Garage Band available for student use. These programs can enhance the projects and bring a new dimension to them.

Computer-Made Graphic Organizer

This is a good beginning of the year assignment to help you learn about your new students while they employ their computer skills and follow specific instructions.

Grades 4–8

Subjects Language Arts, Computer Skills

Time Frame Several lessons

Materials Student copy of the assignment

These are the instructions you will give your students:

Using Word or another program, create a graphic organizer about yourself using the following outline:

1. Name (first and last)
   • 36 point, Bold, Underline
   • center your name

2. Title: Things I Like to Do:
   • 34 point, Bold, Underline, New Font
   • center the title
   • list 3 things related to the title

3. Title: Things I Enjoy Doing With My Family
   • 34 point, Bold, Underline, New Font
   • center the title
   • list 3 things related to the title

4. Title: Favorite Foods
   • 34 point, Bold, Underline, New Font
   • center the title
   • list 3 things related to the title

5. Title: Three Things I Would Like to See This Year
   • 34 point, Bold, Underline, New Font
   • center the title
   • list 3 things related to the title

Attach one appropriate Clip Art image to each section of the Graphic Organizer (for example, an image of a hamburger for the Favorite Food section).

Web Help

A useful website for a "Techtorial" for you or your students: www.education-world.com/a_tech/techtorial/techtorial095.pdf

For middle grades, do some in-class or at-the-computer lessons about fonts and formats as well as keyboard shortcuts and using Clip Art. *For upper grades,* do a refresher lesson before assigning the project.

Musically Inclined

If you have Apple computers in your school, use Garage Band for a project with *upper-grade students.* Students can create a piece of music including a given time signature, number of musical instruments and types of music. A chart and or written summary of the song, including lyrics and settings used, should be completed by each student or group.

The levels in the evaluation rubric could be labeled Platinum, Gold, Silver and Lead, in keeping with traditional record-sales levels.

Book Tie-ins

Picture This! Graphic Organizers by Jennifer Reed

Create a Country

Students can make up their own imaginary country but they have to make it believable.

Grades 5–8

Subjects Geography, Art, Language Arts

Time Frame Several lessons

Materials Atlases and other research materials, paper, coloring materials

Students will make up their own country. Their imaginary country can be placed anywhere in the world, and must use information about the surrounding real countries to determine features such as latitude/longitude, native animals, climate, and so on.

Book Tie-ins

Our World: A Country by Country Guide by Millie Miller

Any student atlas

Lead-up activities to this project include a review of atlas skills and a whole-class study of a chosen country that includes details such as:
- name and meaning
- geographical location
- area
- boundaries and surrounding countries
- landforms
- climate
- native animals and vegetation
- natural resources
- language
- flag
- government
- currency
- time zone

When the class study is complete, students (working individually or in small groups) will create an imaginary country, place it on a world map, and research the same categories used in the class study.

The number of details required for the assignment can vary depending on the grade and ability level of your students. They will use information about the surrounding countries to determine the features of the made-up country. The values they assign to their imaginary country must be plausible when compared with the real surrounding countries.

Each group or individual will produce a poster-sized map with notes and illustrations about their country.

Research Projects

School research projects have evolved a great deal from the traditional animal or country project routinely assigned in the "good old days." Creative methods of presenting information abound. Information itself abounds. The challenge now is to teach students how to locate and synthesize reliable information and to present it in whatever format is required.

A few hints for directing successful student research:

- Make use of your teacher-librarian to help you pre-teach appropriate research skills and to format your project and evaluation method.

- Before you begin, teach students how to keep track of where information came from and to format a bibliography.

- Have students choose a topic based on the availability of resources (check this out ahead of time). Too often students enthusiastically choose a topic only to find a shortage of usable information at their level.

- Always have more books than you have students (so no one gets stuck with the very last one).

- Projects can be done by individuals, partners, groups or the whole class. Vary the groupings throughout the year so that students experience each type of work situation.

- Vary the emphasis for projects. For a traditional research project, stress the process and not the end product by allotting marks for each step of the process and only a small percentage for the end product. For other projects the end product will be the focus.

The traditional research project often uses the SCOPE model to gather and present information

- **Select:** From sources collected and/or overseen by the teacher. These can be books, websites or other sources.

- **Collect:** The taking of point-form notes is a skill that requires explicit teaching followed by guided practice before students are able to proceed on their own. There are several methods for gathering information: students can jot rough notes all on one page then color code them by headings or take point form notes under subheadings.

- **Organize:** Write a rough copy by transcribing rough notes into sentences. Again, guided practice is recommended before working on a project.

- **Present:** Write out/word process a good copy along with a bibliography.

- **Evaluate:** Students receive a rubric at the outset that is used for evaluation. Be sure to add a self-evaluation component that is appropriate for the grade level.

There are numerous other ways to collect and present information: for example, KWHL (what I **know,** what I **want** to find out, **how** I will find out, what I **learned**); and Who, What, When, Where, Why, How.

Web Help

Helpful website: http://www.ri.net/schools/East_Greenwich/research.html#organizing

Desert Island Adventure

Students pretend they are stranded on a desert island and must work in teams to solve problems.

Grades 4–8

Subjects Art, Music, Science, Language Arts, Math

Time Frame One week; time each day depends on how long each activity takes

Materials Coloring materials, Bristol board, materials from home or school to build a simple machine

Before starting the project, have a whole-class discussion about the challenges they would face if stranded without comforts and conveniences. Students will have points of reference based on their familiarity with movies, TV shows and novels on this theme.

Outline the assignment for the class, including the rubric. Divide the students into groups of four to six students.

The assignment can be tailored to the grade level of your students by providing more or less teacher direction as required. For example, in *middle grade classes,* the teacher provides mini lessons or examples for each requirement, and drawing scale maps would not be required; whereas *upper-grade students* would be expected to be more independent in covering the requirements.

In this activity students work as teams on activities and to solve problems that are curriculum based but fit into the desert island scenario.

Day 1: Team building: students think of a motto for their team, design and draw a geometric flag and compose a team jingle.

Day 2: Design a simple machine that will be useful on the island. Depending on the class, you may supply students with materials to use, or have them think of their own.

Day 3: Students create a T-shirt for their team. Teams will create their own logo together. Each child should bring a plain white T-shirt to school and decorate with tie-dye techniques or fabric paint or both.

Day 4: Money or barter: students come up with a system for exchanging money and/or goods. Design and draw their invented currency.

Day 5: Draw a scale map (or create a scale model) of the island.

Each group must also keep an illustrated journal of their activities and experiences with each team member writing at least one entry.

The journal should be presented in a creative way to make it look like it was actually discovered on a deserted island. Journals will be presented to the rest of the class at the conclusion of the project.

Book Tie-ins

Island Trilogy by Gordon Korman

Abel's Island by William Steig (also an animated DVD)

Earth Day Globes

These eye-catching papier-mâché globes can be placed or hung throughout the school with a message on each one about how we can be more earth-friendly.

Grades 3–8

Subjects Science, Art

Time Frame Several lessons

Materials Newspaper torn into strips about 1 inch wide, flour, cold water, boiling water, sugar, paint

Invite parent volunteers to prepare the papier-mâché mixture in the staffroom. No students should be present during that time because of the risk factor of the boiling water.

Have a round balloon blown up and fastened for each student or group. The size of the balloon will determine the size of the finished product. Dip strips of newspaper in the papier mâché, and wrap around the balloon. Let each layer dry before applying the next. Apply several coats.

When the whole thing is dry, sketch in and paint the continents (green) and oceans (blue). Let the paint dry.

Some *middle grade students* may need assistance sketching in the continents. *Upper grade students* will be able to manage on their own.

Possible variations on this project:
- planets/solar system for space study
- pumpkins for a harvest theme
- fish for ocean theme
- snowmen for winter theme

Papier-Mâché Recipe

½ cup all-purpose flour
2 cups cold water
2 cups boiling water
3 tablespoons sugar

Combine ½ cup all-purpose flour and 2 cups cold water in a bowl. Add this mixture to a pot containing 2 cups of boiling water. Bring it to the boil again. Take the pot off the heat and stir in 3 tablespoons of sugar. Cool before using. Mixture will thicken as it cools.

Book Tie-ins

DK First Atlas by DK Publishing
  or any children's atlas

The World Is Flat: Not!
  by W. Frederick Zimmerman

Somewhere in the World Right Now
  by Stacey Schuett

If the World Were a Village by David Smith

Extra Fun Day

A good motivator for students is the promise of a fun event at the end of the month.

Grades K–8

Subjects Any and all

Time Frame One day monthly (or a half day, or whatever works for your classroom)

This is another project that students remember long past their time in your class. Homework completion, good behavior in class and cooperation among students can be the criteria for working toward Extra Fun Day. The class works together to earn the reward and enjoys the benefits of their good work. This one is just plain fun!

Some Extra Fun Day activities:
- wear a hat and chew gum day
- play outside day (winter or summer)
- bring a toy or game from home
- have each student bring a white T-shirt from home and use fabric pens or tie dye to decorate them
- arts and crafts activities
- bring sleeping bags and pillows to school and watch movies
- a "Survivor" style play day with teams and challenges, T-shirts and prizes

- board games day
- a class outing (picnic lunch at a park, skating at a local arena)
- pumpkin carving (in small groups)

A great resource for Extra Fun Day or any day in your classroom is the book *The 175 Best Camp Games*. It provides games of all types for Phys. Ed. class or any time.

Check with parents to see if they are able to facilitate an "extra fun" opportunity. One class had a morning at a curling rink where a parent was a member. Another class had an instructor from a tennis club give a group lesson, and yet another group used the expertise of a school staff member to enjoy some yoga lessons. You'll be surprised at the opportunities a little networking can turn up!

Book Tie-ins

Fun Is a Feeling by Chara M. Curtis

Little Miss Fun by Roger Hargreaves

The 175 Best Camp Games: A Handbook for Leaders by Kathleen, Laura and Mary Fraser

Family Portrait

Students have fun and get an Art lesson creating family portraits.

Grades K–8

Subjects Language Arts

Time Frame Three or more Art lessons

Materials White paper, black construction paper, colored pencils

Spend some time looking at family portraits from art books, personal collections and magazines.

Depending on the grade level, teach some art lessons on any or all of the following: use of detail, background, basic perspective, group placement and any other elements you wish, with a view to having students draw a formal portrait of their family. Have the students draw a rough draft sketch first (on newsprint) and conference with each student about their work and how they can improve it before their good copy.

Present another group lesson on the most common questions or areas of challenge with the rough drafts.

For younger students, have the white paper precut into an oval shape any size you wish the portraits to be. Provide them with a black construction paper frame to glue on top, and have them print "The _____ Family" on a paper tag to be glued to the top or bottom of the frame.

Students in middle and upper grades can cut their own paper and frame after tracing a cardboard template.

The family portrait can be accompanied by a written paragraph, either descriptive in nature (list family members and facts about each), or simply a journal-style piece, again dictated by the grade level of your students.

Parents will treasure these for years!

Book Tie-ins

Simple Pictures Are Best by Nancy Willard

Snapshots From the Wedding by Gary Soto

Families Through the Eyes of Artists (The World of Art Series) by Wendy and Jack Richardson

First Day of School Questionnaire

A great way to get to know a new class is by having them complete sentences that you have started.

Grades 4–8 (can be modified for younger children)

Subjects Language Arts

Time Frame One lesson

Materials Prepared fill-in-the-blank sheet

For this project, prepare a fill-in sheet by starting each sentence, then providing a line or two for student response.

This exercise can provide insight into your new students as they may tell you things on paper that they would not mention in conversation. As well, you get a quick snapshot of a child's penmanship, spelling, pace of working and thought process all on one page!

Modify the project *for younger students* by designing questions that can be answered in one or two words, or by circling or drawing a happy/sad face, or incorporating boxes to check for answers.

First Day of School

Today I feel…
When I grow up…
My family…
No one knows that I…
Everyone knows that I…
I feel happiest when…
A sad time was when…
I think…
A place I would like to visit is…
My house…
Sometimes…
I love to daydream about…
I always…
I never…
My friends like me because…
The best thing I ever did was…
This year I want to…

At the end of the year the same activity with different questions nicely bookends the year and may provide you with some surprises in the "something I never told my teacher until today" department!

Last day of school

The best day of school was…
The worst day of school was…
My favorite subject this year was…
My least favorite subject this year was…
Funniest thing that happened…
Most embarrassing moment…
I'll always remember…
Some important things I learned this year…
Other important things I learned this year
   (not about school)…
Friends this year…
People I got to know better…
Something I got better at this year…
Something I'll have to keep working at
   next year…
Something I never told my teacher about
   (until today)
This summer…
Next year…

Book Tie-ins
(books with multiple responses)
Clive Eats Alligators
  by Alison Lester
When Frank Was Four by Alison Lester
Amazing Anthony Ant
  by Lorna and Graham Philpot

Flat Stanley

The Flat Stanley Project, begun by a Canadian teacher, has been going strong for many years.

Grades K–8

Subjects Art, Language Arts, possibly Science, Math, Social Studies, Music

Time Frame Three- or four-lesson introduction, follow up as required

One of the most well known "teacher project" characters is Flat Stanley, from the book by Jeff Brown. Stanley Lambchop is a character in the book who is flattened when a bulletin board falls on him. Dale Hubert, a Canadian elementary school teacher, began the Flat Stanley Project in 1995 as a means for students to connect with students in other schools.

Web Help

Dale Hubert's Flat Stanley Project can be found at www. flatstanleyproject.com. The website contains a template for making your own Flat Stanley and a signup section for class exchanges.

After reading the book together, students draw and color a paper Flat Stanley and write a journal about the places he goes with the student. Journal entries are then shared within the class and mailed with Flat Stanley to others, who are invited to add to the journal and then return him.

For younger students, a shared writing chart story can be done by the whole class to share Flat Stanley's adventures, and students can work with their families on home-to-school writing.

Middle and upper grade students can work independently and come up with their own ideas for Flat Stanley adventures.

Some famous Flat Stanley moments have been the attendance of "Flat Mark" at the swearing in of Canadian Prime Minister Paul Martin, Arnold Schwarzenegger's appearance with his son's Flat Stanley on the Tonight Show with Jay Leno, and the appearance of

Showcase Projects

Sometimes you need a "wow" project to display in the school. For parent-teacher interview night, open house, education week or other special occasions, these projects give you finished products you and your students will be proud to display.

Art Project
Brown Paper Characters
Choral Reading
Create a Country
Hailstones and Halibut Bones
School Multicultural Project
Sugar Cube Creations
Think Outside the Box

Book Tie-ins

Flat Stanley by Jeff Brown (five other titles in the series)

Mailing May by Michael O. Tunnell and Ted Rand

Mail Myself to You by Woody Guthrie, illustrated by Vera Rosenberry. This is a famous Woody Guthrie song, which can be found on Woody Guthrie CDs or on Fred Penner's *Ebenezer Sneezer* CD.)

Flat Stanley with Olympic athletes at the 2006 Winter Olympics in Torino, Italy.

Students could make a Flat Stanley, photograph him in different locations in the school, and in groups, write about the room that Flat Stanley is in, or photograph him with various textbooks students use and write about what they learn in that subject. Using epals (www.epals.com), teachers can partner with another classroom and exchange information about their respective schools, town or city, or country.

For a more local connection, teachers can partner with another classroom in their school or community and correspond back and forth. If possible, the classes could meet at the end of the project or the school year for a picnic at one school or the other.

Woody Guthrie

An interesting adjunct to this project would be a short study of Woody Guthrie's music and iconic place in folk music history. He lived and sang through the Great Depression and the Dust Bowl era in the United States. Some of his other songs, including "This Land Is Your Land," "Jig Along Home," "Riding In My Car," "Ticky Tock," and "So Long, It's Been Good To Know Ya," are easy to teach and sing.

Folded Paper Art

Your students will enjoy drawing several pictures on a theme, from miniature to HUGE!

Grades 4–8 (can be adapted for younger students)

Subjects Art, Science, Language Arts, Social Studies

Time Frame One or two art lessons

Materials 12-by-18 inch (30 x 45 mm) white paper, crayons, colored pencils, markers

Students are challenged to draw several pictures on a theme, moving from a large 12-by-18 inch size (30 x 45 mm) down to $4\frac{1}{2}$ by 3 inches (7 x $11\frac{1}{2}$ mm).

Choose a theme, for example, animals.

Fold a 12-by-18-inch (30 x 45 mm) piece of white paper in half four times. (For younger students, adapt by using $8\frac{1}{2}$-by-11 paper and folding only twice.)

After unfolding the paper, draw a picture relating to the theme on each fold-out, beginning with smallest or largest space as students choose. Themes *for older students* can be quite specific (for example, mammals), or quite general *for younger students* (for example, animals).

A variation is to have each student choose his or her own theme and have the class guess the theme as students present their finished work, unfolding each section while the other students observe and offer guesses. This project can also be tied in with various curriculum areas; for instance, things related to a unit of study about a person, country, novel study, a Science theme, etc.

A related question is: how many times can you fold a piece of paper? Conventional wisdom says 7, but there have been many articles recently challenging that theory. Check it out on the internet and have a class discussion.

Further investigations into folding can include origami, money folding, the correct way to fold a T-shirt, and napkin folding. Check out the internet for resources.

Book Tie-ins

Folding For Fun: Origami for Ages 4 and Up by Didier Boursin

Folding Paper Fun by Paul Jackson

Friendship Hearts

This community-building exercise asks students to think about the good qualities of their classmates and gives each student the opportunity to be in the spotlight for a day.

Grades K–6

Subjects Language Arts

Time Frame 10 to 15 minutes each day until every student has had a turn. This project works well in February as a Valentine's Day / Friendship celebration.

Materials Construction paper, marker

Choose one student each day and have the class brainstorm that student's good qualities, talents and more. Make a list on the board. Cut a large heart (or whatever shape you choose) out of red or pink construction paper. Write the student's name at the top, then choose three things about the student to write down: one chosen by the student, one chosen by the class (from a list they generate as a group activity) and one chosen by you, the teacher.

Display in the class until each student has a completed heart, then send each student's heart home with the next month's class newsletter or with a covering note from you explaining the process.

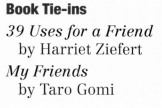

Book Tie-ins

39 Uses for a Friend
 by Harriet Ziefert

My Friends
 by Taro Gomi

Fruit or Vegetable Drawing

This activity focuses student attention on careful observation and detail in drawing. It's simple and effective and makes a great display.

Grades K–8

Subjects Art, Science

Time Frame One or two lessons

Materials A fruit or vegetable brought to school by each student, a knife (to be used by the teacher), a piece of paper divided into three parts, drawing pencils and or watercolors (pencils, paint, or watered-down tempera)

Students will closely examine their fruit or vegetable before it is cut and come up with words to describe it. These can be noted in a journal entry or on a sheet designed by the teacher. After the drawing is complete, students can research facts such as scientific name and meaning, native land, where it is grown today, ideal growing conditions, a few ways it is served, as well as words or sayings, for example, "cool as a cucumber."

The fruit or vegetable will be drawn from three different views:

1. the whole thing
2. cut in half in one direction
3. cut in half in the other direction

This will enable students to observe, compare and contrast the features of the fruit or vegetable, such as texture, seeds, colors and more.

Drawings can then be painted using watercolors or watered-down tempera paint.

Book Tie-ins

A Fruit Is a Suitcase for Seeds
  by Jean Richards

Growing Vegetable Soup
  by Lois Ehlert

Outside-Inside: Sweet Sour Juicy
  by Eleonore Schmid

The ABCs of Fruits and Vegetables and Beyond by Steve Charney and David Goldbeck

Eating the Alphabet by Lois Ehlert

Graduated Page-Length Book

Young children love cumulative stories, in which each time a new event occurs, all the previous events are repeated. Cumulative stories lend themselves well to this project.

Grades K–4

Subjects Language Arts, Art

Time Frame Several lessons

Materials Premade booklets with graduated page-lengths for students to write and draw in. Tailor the number of pages in the booklet to the number of events you want the students to write about. A useful website with directions for making "step" booklets is www.makingbooks.com/freeprojects.shtml.

Choose a story that has a series of events. Read the story to the students and study the book using Shared Reading strategies.

The students will write and illustrate each event in the series on a separate page of the booklet. The first page is the shortest and every following page should be a bit longer than the previous one. Students can also make up their own stories and illustrate them.

Book Tie-ins

Stone Soup (there are many versions of this story)

The House That Jack Built (also many versions)

There Was an Old Lady Who Swallowed a Fly (again, many versions)

Henny Penny (numerous versions)

Today Is Monday by Eric Carle

The Jacket I Wear in the Snow by Shirley Neitzel (this author has an entire series of cumulative stories)

Shoes from Grandpa by Mem Fox

Building a Class Library

There are many ways to accumulate a great classroom collection.

- Start with your principal and ask for money to build your class library.

- Borrow books from your school or public library on current units of study and have these books available for students. (To avoid fines or lost items, books from the public library borrowed under the teacher's names should not be taken home by the students.)

- Ask parents for donations of gently used books in either your class newsletter or the school newsletter.

- Use accumulated credits from classroom book programs such as Scholastic Book Clubs to enhance your collection.

- Visit a few garage sales on Saturday mornings.

- Used book stores often have inexpensive hidden treasures.

- If your school has a book fair, have a "wish list" available for each classroom so that parents who wish to buy and donate a book may do so.

- In lieu of holiday gifts for the teacher, ask for book store gift certificates you can use to add to your classroom library.

Group Share After Reading

This activity takes daily reading time to the next level. Sharing, wondering and noticing lead the group into rich discussions.

Grades K–8

Subjects Language Arts

Time Frame Can be a few minutes each day, a once-a-week activity or any schedule that fits your class

Most classrooms have a "quiet reading" time. It goes by different names, for instance, SSR (Sustained Silent Reading) or DEAR (Drop Everything And Read), but the aim is the same: to have students reading self-selected books, to have the whole class (including the teacher) reading together, and to nurture the love of reading, not just in the classroom, but for lifelong learning.

After quiet reading time, open up a time for discussion. Initially the discussion will need to be guided by the teacher, who begins by giving an example from her own reading or from a book she is reading to the class. As students become familiar with the process, they will come up with their own discussion starters. The direction discussions take will amaze you!

Students share with the class something they have noticed or liked or wondered about in their books. It could be a bit of dialogue, something about the writer's style, or a question ("What is an epilogue?") or anything else they choose.

One way to begin and to clearly illustrate the type of discussion you are looking for is to read a picture book or short story to the class, and have a practice sharing session with everyone talking about the same book.

Encourage student participation in response to peer comments. Teachers can track each student's level of participation by making quick anecdotal notes about who takes part in discussion and a one- or two-word note about the topics brought up. Students reluctant to take part can be given a few days' notice that their turn will be coming up, so they can prepare something in advance.

Results of these discussions can be used to plan mini lessons in reading or writing, to guide students' independent reading choices and to consolidate text-to-text, text-to-self and text-to-world connection-making.

Another benefit of group share time is that students will become curious about books that other students are talking about. In one Grade 4 class a student with an interest in the classics started a run on the genre; the teacher had to stock the classroom with enough junior classic versions of novels to satisfy the demand!

Sample anecdotal notes taken during group share time:

Ryan: Martin Luther King biography, shared pictures

Elisa: *Island of the Blue Dolphins*, summary of the chapter she is reading right now, good oral retelling

Devin: his brother knows the Martin Luther King speech "I Have a Dream"

Liam: *Fly Away Home* (novelization of movie) has seen the movie

Michaela: knew that William Lishman, who the character of the father in *Fly Away Home* was based on, has written his own book called *Father Goose*

Renee: her book has an epilogue, wondered what that was

Hailstones and Halibut Bones

Students tap their most creative selves as they explore Mary O'Neill's poems about color and create their own pattern poems.

Grades 4–8 (can be adapted for younger grades)

Subjects Language Arts, Art

Time Frame One to two weeks

Mary O'Neill's classic book of poetry, *Hailstones and Halibut Bones: Adventures in Color,* published in 1961, is a lovely foray into all the colors of the spectrum. Do some thinking exercises with the group. Brainstorm a list for the color gray following the template at the top of the next page in a large format. Work with the class as a whole to fill in the blanks. Encourage detailed and imaginative responses.

Share the poem "What is Gray?" from O'Neill's book with the class by putting it on an overhead or a chart. Talk about its structure, use of the senses, and how it paints pictures with words. Emphasize the fine detail of O'Neill's writing: the similes,

alliteration, focus on texture and precise, yet creative description. A few preparatory mini-lessons on these writing tools in the week before this project would be helpful for students. Encourage students to really feel the color, to reach within for unique ways of expressing themselves.

Divide the class into groups and assign each group a color. Students can be given an organizational template to help them structure their ideas. Each group will produce a poem, loosely modeled on "What is Gray?"

Poems should be written over a period of several days and then edited, compiled and bound, or made into large illustrated posters. When class poems are complete and have been presented, share the rest of Mary O'Neill's poems with the class. Compare and contrast the students' work with the originals.

An extension to this project is for two teachers who teach the same grade to do this project with their respective classes, then come together to present the finished products (for example, perhaps one color a day for a period of time). For full immersion into the world of color, students could be invited to wear clothing in the "color of the day."

This project also lends itself to a scientific exploration/explanation of color, as well as some lessons on blending colors, the rainbow, or the color wheel.

GROUP MEMBERS: _____

OUR COLOR: _____

SHADES OF OUR COLOR: _____

EXAMPLES OF THINGS THAT ARE OUR COLOR:

TASTE _____ SMELL _____

TOUCH_____ FEELINGS _____

SOUNDS_____

EXPERIENCES _____

_____

Book Tie-ins

Hailstones and Halibut Bones by Mary O'Neill, illustrated by John Wallner. The original version is now out of print, but can be bought inexpensively on used bookstore websites or found in public and school libraries. The John Wallner version is still in print and readily available.

All the Colors of the Earth by Sheila Hamanaka

Black Is Brown Is Tan by Arnold Adoff

Color Me a Rhyme: Nature Poems For Young People by Jane Yolen

Why Is an Orange Called an Orange? by Cobi Ladner

The Science Book of Color by Neil Ardley

Hear and Draw

Students use their imaginations to create a drawing that represents their own view of a book that is read to them.

Grades K–8

Subjects Art, Language Arts

Time Frame One or two lessons

Materials A book to read to the class, white paper, crayons, colored pencils, markers

From time to time we watch a movie based on a book we have read. Our reaction is often "that's not how I pictured it/her/him/them at all!" In this project, students will filter the words of a book through their imaginations to come up with a drawing that represents their view of a book that you read to them.

This project can be done with any grade level and book, but a good one to start for middle grades and up is *Two Bad Ants* by Chris Van Allsburg. Before reading the story to students (without showing the pictures or cover of the book), have students fold a paper into eight sections, and number them 1 to 8. (Depending on your grade level, you could use six or four sections instead of eight.)

Read the story twice. The first time, students listen and do not write. During the second reading, students write one important point from the story in each box. They will then draw a picture to go with each of the captions, a sketch at first, followed by a conference with the teacher to edit and check the rough copy and then a good copy.

When all are finished, read the story again, this time showing the illustrations. Discuss similarities/differences between student and author illustrations.

For *younger students*, a single picture may be drawn after listening to the story. To guide the students' listening, ask them to concentrate on one character or image from the story in the second reading. *Middle grades* could do four pictures, and *older students* could do six or eight pictures, depending on your students.

Book Tie-ins

Two Bad Ants by Chris Van Allsburg

Lyle, Lyle, Crocodile
by Bernard Waber

Good Dog, Carl by Alexandra Day

When I Was Young in the Mountains
by Cynthia Rylant

*Taking a Bath with the Dog
and Other Things that Make
Me Happy*
by Scott Menchin

The 100-Square Learning Carpet

The 100-square learning carpet is a floor carpet with 100 squares. It is an effective tool for active learning as students physically place and move objects on the carpet. It can be used for all Math strands: numeration, patterning, measurement, patterning, data management and probability, as well as language and mapping skills. Activities can be done by the whole class, groups or individuals. Visual and kinesthetic learners benefit from seeing concepts demonstrated on the carpet in cooperative learning situations. Using the carpet to teach or review concepts provides students with an opportunity to gain confidence and practice before moving on to individual pencil and paper tasks. Check out www.thelearningcarpet.ca for more ideas.

Hibernation Day

Midwinter is a great time for this day of celebration and the lead-up to it.

Grades K–3

Subjects Science, Drama, Music, Art, Language Arts, Phys. Ed., Math

Time Frame A day or part of a day following a unit of study

Materials A large flat sheet to make a "cave" (be creative: push bookcases together and drape a sheet over top, use tables, coat-hanging area, etc.), white foam cups, brown paint

After studying animals in winter, seasonal changes, or animal adaptations, arrange a special day (or part of the day, depending on your schedule) to consolidate learning and experience some fun activities. Activities can be done in centers or as a large group.

Possible activities:

- Children dress in pajamas or cozy clothes and bring a stuffed animal to school.

- Bring in a large flat sheet. Drape it over bookshelves, children's cubby area or wherever you can make a "cave." Invite children in four or five at a time to read quietly.

- Serve hot chocolate and cookies at snack time.
- Read books about animals that hibernate.
- A hibernating bear craft: teacher cuts white foam cups in half lengthwise. Paint both sides of the cup brown (best done one day ahead). Glue onto a square of brown (for earth color) or white (for snow color) Bristol board, cut side down to resemble a cave. Cotton balls can be glued onto a white base to represent snow. Glue some straw onto the floor of the cave and use a large brown pompom to represent the sleeping bear.
- Play games such as Hibernation Rhyming. Students pretend to sleep, and the teacher says two words. If words do not rhyme, children stay asleep; if they do rhyme, wake up.
- Teach and sing *Time for Hibernation* song.
- Animal puppets can be used to make up and act out short plays about hibernation.
- Color pictures of animal that hibernate.
- Watch a non-fiction movie about hibernation or storybook bears.
- Use stuffed animals that students have brought in to make a line organized from shortest to tallest animal.
- Measure bears using non-standard (for example, cubes) or standard measurement depending on grade level.
- Graph the number of each type of stuffed animal brought in by students (use a hundred square learning carpet or pocket chart).

Time for Hibernation
(to the tune of *"Frère Jacques"*)

Are you sleeping, are you sleeping,
Big black bear, big black bear?
Time for hibernation. What is your location?
In a log, in a lair.

Are you sleeping, are you sleeping,
Hanging bat, hanging bat?
Time for hibernation. What is your location?
In a cave is where I'm at.

Are you sleeping, are you sleeping,
Garter snake, garter snake?
Time for hibernation. What is your location?
In the mud, in a lake.

Are you sleeping, are you sleeping,
Toad and frog, toad and frog?
Time for hibernation. What is your location?
In a pond, near a log.

Are you sleeping, are you sleeping,
Meadow mouse, meadow mouse?
Time for hibernation. What is your location?
In a field, near a house.

Are you sleeping, are you sleeping,
Turtle friend, turtle friend?
Time for hibernation. What is your location?
In the stream, till winter's end!

(from www.littlegiraffes.com)

Book Tie-ins
Hibernation by Margaret Hall
Wake Me in Spring by James Preller
Time to Sleep by Denise Fleming
DK Readers: A Bed for Winter by DK Publishing
How Do Bears Sleep? by E. J. Bird

It Looked Like Spilt Milk

In this activity based on the book It Looked Like Spilt Milk, students will make their own "cloud" and write about it what it looks like.

Grades K–6

Subjects Art, Science

Time Frame One lesson for looking at clouds outdoors, one lesson for learning about types of clouds in the classroom, one lesson to make the clouds, one lesson to present

Materials White paper, sky blue construction paper, glue

Most of us have at one time or another looked up at clouds in the sky and thought about how a certain cloud looked like an animal or an object. Students make their own "cloud" and write about what it looks like in this activity based on the book *It Looked Like Spilt Milk.*

Plan this activity for a party cloudy day when the class can go outside to observe cloud shapes. Sit (or even lie on the ground) with your students and observe the various cloud shapes, and challenge students to tell you what the cloud shapes remind them of.

Back in the classroom, read the book *It Looked Like Spilt Milk.* Discuss. Give each child an 8½-x-11-inch piece of white paper that is folded in half. Have the students carefully tear the paper into a shape, being careful to leave at least a part of the folded side intact. When they have finished tearing the shape, open the paper and look at it from all sides and angles. When the students look at their paper, they should be able to imagine what it looks like to them.

Glue the white shape onto sky blue construction paper (in the book it is dark blue, but light blue would work as well) and write the words "Sometimes it looked like _____" under the shape. Kindergarten students may need you to scribe for them.

Compile all the pages into a class book. Complete the book by making a final page the same as the original "Sometimes it looked like spilt milk. But it wasn't spilt milk. It was just a cloud in the sky."

The book can be sent home with a different student each night to be shared with families.

Book Tie-ins

It Looked Like Spilt Milk
    by Charles G. Shaw

The Book of Clouds
    by John A. Day

Little Cloud by Eric Carle

Cloud Dance by Thomas Locker

The Cloud Book by Tomie de Paola

The Man Who Named the Clouds by Julie Hannah

The Kids' Book of Clouds and Sky by Frank Staub

Clouds (Watts Library) by Trudi Strain Trueit

Leaf Pictures

First get some fresh air, then get to work on a picture using leaves collected in your neighborhood.

Grades K–8

Subjects Art

Time Frame One or two art lessons

Materials Construction paper or Bristol board for background, an assortment of leaves, glue, colored pencils, or markers

Share the book *Look What I Did With a Leaf* by Morteza E. Sohi with students. Discuss various pictures that can be made with leaves. If possible, go for a class walk to gather leaves in all sizes, shapes and colors. Press the leaves under books or something heavy overnight. After a day or two, have a look at some of the leaves with the class. Ask if the colors or shapes suggest an animal, or an object.

Have students choose leaves and create a picture with them. Older students should be expected to create a much more detailed picture than younger ones. Markers or pencil crayons can be used to add details. Laminate for strength.

Using a field guide for trees and leaves that is specific to your area, identify the various leaves you have collected. Make a bulletin board display or chart showing the leaf and the name of the tree it comes from.

Book Tie-ins

Look What I Did With a Leaf
  by Morteza E. Sohi

Leaf Man
  by Lois Ehlert

Red Leaf, Yellow Leaf by Lois Ehlert

I Am a Leaf
  by Jean Marzollo

Fun With Leaves Stencils
  (Dover Little Activity Book)

Fandex Family Field Guide: Trees by Steven Aronson

Leaf Project

Students create a booklet in which they record their scientific and mathematical findings in this interactive leaf study.

Grades K–2 (can be adapted for use in higher grades)

Subjects Science, Math, Language Arts

Time Frame 20 minutes per day for as long as it takes to complete the booklet, or one longer session organized into centers

Materials One leaf per student, crayons or pencil crayons, cubes for measuring, a container filled with pennies, a medium-sized bowl or container filled with water

If possible, go for a class walk to gather leaves in all sizes, shapes and colors. If you are not using the leaves the same day they are collected, press them under books or something heavy overnight. Leaves collected from the walk in the previous project can also be used for this interactive leaf study.

The following day, have each student choose a leaf and complete these activities, which could be done in centers or by the whole class. Each child can work in a booklet prepared by the teacher. *In Kindergarten,* one activity per day could be teacher directed and supervised.

- Tape the leaf onto the front of the recording booklet after all activities are finished.
- Make a detailed drawing of the leaf on a page inside the booklet. Do a little mini lesson beforehand on how to look closely at a leaf and observe its features and details.

Other pages in the booklet can show the results of the following activities:

- Measure how many cubes tall the leaf is (non-standard units of measurement for younger grades, ruler for older grades).
- Cover the leaf completely with pennies (introduction to area) and write down how many pennies it takes.
- Float the leaf in a container of water and place pennies on it one at a time. Write down how many pennies it will hold before sinking.
- Write words that describe the leaf (color, size, shape).
- Drop the leaf from over your head and count how many seconds pass before the leaf touches the ground.

Book Tie-ins
Fall Leaf Project
by Margaret McNamara

License Plates

Students will think of and design a personalized license plate, measure, cut, draw and color the plate.

Grades 4–8

Subjects Math, Art

Time Frame Two or three art lessons

Materials Heavy white paper, rulers, scissors, pencil crayons or markers the same color as the license plate letters and numbers in your province or state

Before starting the project, search online or call the department of motor vehicles or license bureau in your area. Get information from them regarding requirements for personalized plates. Have students follow these requirements in their designs.

In class, talk about the license plates in your state or province. Note the color, size and symbols on the plates. Discuss the difference between "regular" and personalized plates. Have students design a personalized license plate that they would like to have on a car, for someone they know or for a famous person.

Do a lesson on measurement, that is, measuring the height/width/spacing of letters and numbers on the plates.

Depending on grade level, distribute paper cut to the right dimensions or have the children measure and cut. Sketch in the letters/numbers lightly in pencil, then color and outline.

When license plates are completed, display them in the class or in the library. If possible, take the completed plates to a local license bureau (at an off-peak time) and determine which of the students' plate designs could legally be used.

Have students do online research about license plates in other parts of your country and in countries around the world (note color, shape, etc.) Compile a class chart of your findings. There are lots of interesting plates out there such as Wyoming's brown bronco and Canada's Northwest Territories polar bear shape.

Web Help

www.worldlicenseplates.com

Book Tie-ins

Nifty Plates from the Fifty States
by Paul Beatrice

The Way Cool License Plate Book
by Leonard Wise

*What Does That Mean?
The Personal Stories Behind
Vanity License Plates*
by Dennis R. Cowhey

Math Olympics

An interactive Mathematics session where students work as a team to solve problems correctly faster than other teams.

Grades 3–8

Subjects Math

Time Frame Set a time that you feel is appropriate for the grade level.

Materials 10 math questions for your grade level copied and laid out in 10 stations around the classroom, answer sheet, score sheet

Write about 10 math questions including material from every strand. Be sure to have logic questions, computation and problem-solving. The questions should vary in difficulty and complexity according to grade level. Number each question. Make four or five copies of each question about the size/shape of a recipe card. Have a sheet at your desk with the answers on it that is clearly laid out for you to see, but that the runners

cannot see. Also have a score sheet for each team close at hand. An 8½-by-11-inch page separated into boxes (one per team) with the numbers 1 to 10 in each box works well as a score sheet. Put an X through each question as the team presents you with the correct answer.

Arrange 10 centers around the room. Place copies of Question 1 at Center 1, Question 2 at Center 2, and so on. Ensure that the centers are not too close together. (A desk pulled off to the side of the room will function adequately.)

Divide the class into teams. Try to have three to four students per team, and try to have students with a variety of ability levels working together. Number of teams will vary depending how many students you have in your class. Each team will have a designated area of the class in which to work. Have the team pick *one* runner. Only the designated

runner can go get a question from a center and that same person is the only one who can come to your desk to check the answer. This cuts down on confusion and you get used to seeing the same face for a certain team.

The teams can work at the centers in whatever order they choose. If they get a question that they can't solve, they can put it back and get another one, but each team can only work on one question at a time. If the runner comes to your desk for an answer check and has the wrong answer, the team may try again.

Students may use whatever materials they need to find the answer (toothpicks, poker chips, cubes or any other math manipulatives you have in the classroom). A question that needs a calculator will not be a straightforward, easy calculation, but more of a logic question.

Set a time limit, and the team with the most correct answers wins. It's wild and crazy and so much fun.

This activity can be interactive between classes at the same grade level. The winning team from each class or grade level can be declared and the recognized at divisional or whole-school assembly, complete with Math Olympic medals or ribbons. Teachers can coordinate the timing of this activity so that the whole school holds Math Olympics at the same time of year. Many school districts have Math competitions and contests that students can be encouraged to enter based on the interest sparked by this activity.

Book Tie-ins

The Secret Life of Math
  by Ann McCallum

Math Curse
  by Jon Scieszka

The Grapes of Math
  by Greg Tang

Monthly Newsletter Written by the Class

Students create a monthly newsletter about curriculum and class events to bring school life home to parents.

Grades K–8

Subjects Language Arts, Media Studies

Time Frame One to three lessons

Materials Supplies for writing and publishing

Many teachers are required to write a monthly newsletter to communicate with parents about curriculum and class events. Contributions by students make it more likely that students will give the newsletter to parents and ensure that it is read by the family, and they make it more interactive. The feedback generated by student-written newsletter entries will also give the teacher a sense of what students are taking away from the units being taught in the classroom.

Once a month, brainstorm on the board a list of subjects and the current unit being studied. Have students work in pairs to write a paragraph on what the class is studying in various subjects, for example, Reading, Writing, Library, Math, Art, whole school events, field trips or any other areas of interest.

The teacher can write an opening message and include articles or pictures by the students. Parents will enjoy reading what the students have written, and it gives students an authentic purpose for writing.

This can also be an individual activity where students write a journal entry after a group brainstorming session. Teachers can use the journal entries to assess student writing and to gauge student reaction to the unit content and activities.

To adapt the project *for younger grades,* you could pick a certain number of students to draw pictures or write the words for headings each month so that each student has a turn before the end of the year.

You could also add student quotes about what they have learned or have them draw pictures to accompany text written by other students or teachers.

A Note on Multiple Intelligences

Lessons and projects become more meaningful when you plan with various learning styles in mind. Here are some ways to incorporate the eight intelligences into classroom activities.

Bodily-Kinesthetic / Body Smart

- gym class
- creative movement
- performing
- building
- manipulatives
- simulations
- changing classroom arrangement
- dancing

Interpersonal / People Smart

- drama
- cooperative learning activities (jigsaw, think/pair/share)
- peer teaching, editing or tutoring
- cross-age teaching, editing or tutoring
- sharing
- partner, small or large group work
- class discussions
- brainstorming

Intrapersonal / Self Smart

- personal response journal
- independent projects
- self reflection/assessment
- goal setting
- metacognition (thinking about what you are thinking)
- self-talk

Logical-Mathematical / Number Smart

- graphic organizers
- critical thinking
- experiments
- collecting data
- predicting
- Venn diagrams
- puzzles
- logic games

Musical / Music Smart

- playing background music
- playing instruments
- singing
- keeping rhythm
- musical games
- hum, rap, tap

Naturalist / Nature Smart

- using a microscope
- nature walk
- identifying
- classifying
- growing plants
- labeling
- studying patterns

Verbal-Linguistic / Word Smart

- storytelling
- choral speaking
- public speaking
- listening
- dramatizing
- presenting
- retelling

Visual-Spatial / Picture Smart

- illustrate
- 3D projects
- graphic organizers
- creating a piece of art
- visualizing
- collages/murals
- filming
- color coding

See the next page for a Multiple Intelligences Booklet project.

Multiple Intelligences Booklet

The theory of multiple intelligences was proposed by Howard Gardner in 1983. Most educators are familiar with its content, and many teachers use it in their classrooms to help each child maximize their potential and self-awareness. Students will surprise you as they assemble their booklets with how well they know themselves and their talents.

Grades 3–8

Subjects Language Arts, possibly Math

Time Frame Two to three lessons

Materials Photocopied sheet that names and explains each type of intelligence, scissors, construction paper to make a cover, pencil crayons, stapler

Talk about the theory of multiple intelligences at a level appropriate for the grade. Make or purchase a poster showing the eight intelligences with words and pictures illustrating the attributes of each. See page 77.

Give students a photocopied sheet with the eight intelligences on it (smaller version of the large poster). Have them cut each intelligence out and glue it on a piece of construction paper in order as the student sees him/herself, from strongest intelligence to weakest.

Another option is to make a booklet by measuring and cutting out and illustrating construction paper covers.

Older students can make their own booklet from scratch, writing and illustrating a page for each intelligence, putting them in order, and making a cover for their booklet. Depending on grade level, they could accompany this with a journal entry explaining their choices, and/or present to the class.

If students are presenting to each other, stick to a format where each student reveals only their strongest area. This will build self-confidence and community among students.

For younger grades, the theory of multiple intelligences can be introduced and elaborated upon in a less formal way. Teachers can emphasize throughout the year that everyone has things that they are good at and things they struggle with. A simple poster can be made or purchased and displayed in the classroom.

Book Tie-ins

*Frames of Mind:
The Theory of Multiple
Intelligences*
by Howard Gardner

7 Kinds of Smart
by Thomas Armstrong

*You're Smarter than You Think: A Kid's
Guide to Multiple Intelligences*
by Thomas Armstrong

The Mysteries of Harris Burdick

The Mysteries of Harris Burdick is a mystery book composed of exquisite black-and-white drawings, each with a title and a tag line, that practically beg to be written about.

Grades 4–8

Subjects Language Arts, Art

Time Frame One introductory lesson, several sessions for writing and editing

Materials A copy of *The Mysteries of Harris Burdick*, writing and publishing materials

Web Help

The Harris Burdick website, www.themysteriesofharrisburdick.com, contains teacher tips, reader's stories, an opportunity to submit stories and a couple of animations and songs inspired by the illustrations.

In 1984, the incomparable Chris Van Allsburg published *The Mysteries of Harris Burdick*. The book's beautiful illustrations are available in a portfolio edition containing loose, oversize sheets perfect for display in the classroom.

The book begins with a letter from Chris Van Allsburg to the reader. It contains a challenge: to take inspiration from the drawings and to make up stories to accompany them. Once the students see the drawings the lesson practically runs itself. Students may choose the drawing that intrigues them the most as the basis for their story. Follow your usual class procedure for writing, editing and sharing.

A great follow-up to the story writing is an Art lesson using charcoal pencils or sticks.

Book Tie-ins

The Mysteries of Harris Burdick by Chris Van Allsburg

Any of Chris Van Allsburg's other books

Book Tie-ins

The book tie-ins for each project are a starting point to which you will add your own choices of material to share with your students. Spend some time exploring your school library, work with your teacher-librarian, get to know a children's librarian at your public library, and be on the lookout for music, poetry, news stories and personal experiences that you can add to what you are teaching in the classroom.

Talk is essential and connections are everywhere. Your students will bring dimensions to class discussions that will amaze you. Over the course of the year you will build a culture of shared references in discussions with your students. This will be the scaffold upon which they will stand to think, connect, create and become lifelong learners.

Page One

Students learn how to read with awareness when they closely examine the first page of a story.

Grades 3–8

Subjects Language Arts

Time Frame One or two lessons each time

Materials Photocopied page of a short story or novel for each student

To introduce this activity, show an overhead of the first page of a previously unread book and, as a class, brainstorm ideas for what they discover about the story from that page. Write student ideas informally right on the overhead using arrows, circles or underlining to point out words or phrases of interest. Students may also contribute questions, or things they wonder about on the basis of that first page.

After doing a couple of group sessions, repeat the activity with either a small group or individually using a different first page.

The selection you use should not be chosen in isolation, but should be a book you will go on to read to the class, a book that will be used for a novel study or a book that will be used in some other way in the classroom.

When students work in small groups or on their own, they may circle words, write in the margin, explain their thoughts in point form or sentences.

This is a good way for students to focus their thoughts about a new story or book, to have questions in their mind as they read, and read with awareness.

This method also works well at the beginning of an individual novel study. Photocopy the first page of each student's novel and instruct them to write their responses on the page.

To adapt for younger grades, use the first page of a big book and record student responses on the board, on sticky notes or simply discuss. Concentrate on directing students to what they can tell by looking at the pictures, hearing the words, and using what they see and hear to make predictions about the rest of the book.

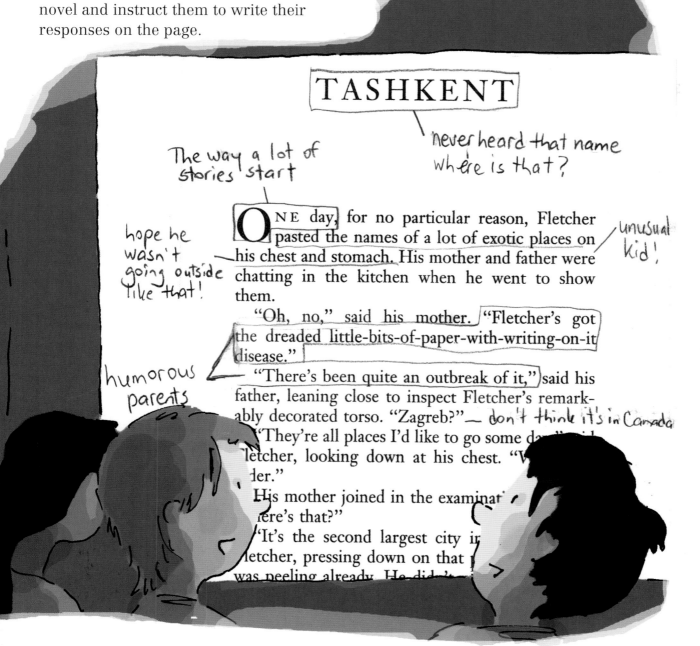

Planet Walk

The vastness of the solar system is mind-boggling. Set up a scale model using everyday items for the Sun and planets.

Grades 1–8 (the complexity of the lesson will vary according to your grade level)

Subjects Science, Math, Art

Time Frame A couple of lessons to introduce the topic and set up the experiment, one session to set up your mini solar system and a couple of lessons for follow-up activities

Materials For a 1,000 Yard Solar System, a large outdoor space, perhaps a sidewalk outside the school and down the street, objects to represent the Sun and planets. A 100 Yard Solar System can likely be done inside the school gym.

  Sun: a ball 8 inches (approximately 20 cm) in diameter
  Mercury: a pinhead
  Venus: a peppercorn
  Earth: a peppercorn
  Mars: a pinhead
  Jupiter: a chestnut
  Saturn: a hazelnut or acorn
  Uranus: a peanut or coffee bean
  Neptune: a peanut or coffee bean
  Pluto: a pinhead

A way to give students an idea of the mind-boggling size of the solar system is to set up a scale model using everyday items. Follow the directions given in any of the many websites on this subject. Do a search for 1000 Yard Solar System and find one that works for you and your students.

There are also websites that describe a 100 Yard Solar System that will fit into a more compact space.

Prepare the students for this activity by studying basic facts about the solar system. Reviewing the concept of scale and doing some preliminary class work will make the lesson easier to understand. Explain to the students what the activity will entail, and prepare all the materials.

Put a small group of students in charge of each planet. Pick a starting point, place the "Sun" in position on the ground and march off the paces as follows:

Mercury: 10 paces from Sun
Venus: 9 paces from Mercury
Earth: 7 paces from Venus
Mars: 14 paces from Earth
Jupiter: 95 paces from Mars
Saturn: 112 paces from Jupiter
Uranus: 249 paces from Saturn
Neptune: 281 paces from Uranus
Pluto: 242 paces from Neptune

Placing the objects on a card will make them easier to find when retracing your steps back to the Sun.

If you have next to no space for this activity, a very small model can still be made using the relative distances listed here. For a smaller model, mark off the planets in units of 1 inch or 1 centimeter instead of 1 pace; so, for instance, Mercury is 10 inches from the Sum, Venus is 9 inches from Mercury, and so on.

Follow-up activities can involve research on the planets, lessons on the orbit of planets, and more. The solar system is the limit!

Book Tie-ins

How Big Is a Million?
by Anna Milborne

How Much Is a Million?
by David M. Schwartz
and Steven Kellogg

Play Dough Predictor

This is great take-home on the first day of school for young students. Prepare at home and have the bags ready to give out at the end of the day.

Grades K–2

Subjects Language Arts, Math

Time Frame One or two lessons

Materials Flour, salt, water, vegetable oil, cream of tartar, food coloring, photocopied poem

Make play dough using this tried-and-true recipe.

3 cups flour
1½ cups salt
3 cups water
2 tbsp. vegetable oil
1 tbsp. cream of tartar
Food coloring (3 different colors)

Mix all the ingredients together except for the food coloring. Stir over medium heat for about 5 minutes, or until the mixture does not stick to the sides of the pan and forms a ball. Turn the mixture out onto a cutting board, cool slightly, then knead until smooth. Roll the play dough into small ball (about 1 inch across). Poke a hole in the ball and put two or three drops of food coloring in the hole.

Make play dough balls with three different colors inside. This lends itself to follow-up activities the next day. Form the play dough back into a ball again, covering the drops of food coloring. Place each ball into a zip lock bag, and add a copy of this little poem, with the student's name on it.

Here's your play dough, round and white
When you squeeze, it, what a sight!
If it turns a color, give a cheer
It means we'll have a great school year!

Give students the bag at the very end of the day and ask them to take it home, and *not* to squeeze it until they are with their parents. Parents can read the poem to the children, then supervise the child as they squeeze the ball and watch what happens. Children then squeeze the ball with parent supervision and watch what happens.

The children will be so excited to return to school the next day and tell you what color they got!

Results can then be graphed using a concrete graph on a 100-square learning carpet (see page 65), a large graph on the board or a chart, or on individual graphs by students at their places.

Grades 1 and 2 students could also write about and draw a picture of the experience while *Kindergarten students* could draw a picture and have the teacher scribe their words.

Play Money Spelling Bee

Traditional spelling bees favor naturally good spellers and can be intimidating to many students, but this one works on a team approach where every student can be a valuable contributor.

Grades 1–8

Subjects Language Arts, Math

Time Frame Set a time limit that is appropriate for your grade level.

Materials List of easy, medium and difficult words, class Math materials, and $1, $5 and $10 bills from a game, or make your own play money designed for your class (designing the money for this activity could be an Art activity culminating in a vote by the students for their favorite currency).

Prepare a list of $1 (easy), $5 (medium) and $10 (difficult) words for your grade level. Many spelling texts have all the List Words in alphabetical order at the back of the book. This is a good resource to use for making the list.

Divide students into teams. Try to have four to five students on a team so they do not have to wait too long for their turn. Appoint a banker for each team to handle the money. That student holds and keeps track of the team's dollar amount.

Each student may choose the dollar level he wants to try when his turn comes. Most students have a pretty good idea of their own ability level, and can choose the right level for themselves.

Explain to the students that it is better to

pick a $1 word and get it right than to try a $10 word and get it wrong. Play until each student has had a turn and/or set a time limit. The first few times you play, just run through each team once, then as they get used to the game they will ask to play for a longer time.

No one is ever "out," even if they miss a word. After each turn, students go to the end of the line to await their next turn.

The team with the most money at the end of the time is the winner. Invite students to cheer each other on, but no help may be given to team members.

Book Tie-ins

The Berenstain Bears and the Big Spelling Bee by Jan Berenstain and Mike Berenstain

Poetry Circle

This works well as a first activity after introducing a poetry unit.

Grades 3–8

Subjects Language Arts, Drama, Art

Time Frame One or two introductory lessons, followed by one poetry circle sharing session per week for three or four weeks

Materials A large selection of poetry books

Introduce the poetry unit in your classroom by sharing poems with students. Amass a collection of poetry books from your school, public and or class library. Be sure to have more books than you have students. Try to have a large selection of poetic styles.

For your introductory lesson, share four or five poems with students, perhaps on an overhead or a photocopied sheet so they can follow along. Discuss the poems, elicit responses from the students and whet their poetic appetites.

In the days following, do book talks on the poetry books you have in the class.

Ask each student to browse the books and locate a poem that appeals to him or her. Tell students to learn to read their poems with expression or memorize them for presentation to the class. Actions may be added. Students should also write a response journal entry about the poem.

On poem presentation day, students sit in a circle and take turns presenting their chosen poem to the class. Depending on the grade level, size, and attention span of your students, have only a certain number of presentations per day. Have a group sharing session after each day's presentations to encourage students to share thoughts, feelings or questions about the poems. Anyone in the group may answer or respond. Before beginning the presentations, have a guided practice sharing session to model your expectations.

After a few weeks of poetry circle, when each student has had a chance to present three to four poems, have each student choose the poem that he/she has enjoyed the most and create a work of art that expresses his/her feelings about the poem.

In the upper grades students can also research the poet's life and work and write up a short report. For older students who may be less than thrilled about studying poetry, check out the work of Michael Rosen.

Getting a Start in Poetry

The books of Georgia Heard, poet and teacher, are an excellent guide for introducing your students (and perhaps yourself) to the joys of poetry. Her approach integrates poetry into the lives of children in a simple, yet powerful way.

For the Good of the Earth and Sun: Teaching Poetry by Georgia Heard

Awakening the Heart: Exploring Poetry in Elementary and Middle School by Georgia Heard

Book Tie-ins

Eenie Meenie Manitoba by Robert Heidbreder, illustrated by Scot Ritchie

Poems for the Very Young selected by Michael Rosen

The Random House Book of Poetry for Children selected by Jack Prelutzky

Any book of poetry by Shel Silverstein

Any book of poetry by Jack Prelutsky

Poetry Speaks to Children edited by Elise Paschen (includes a CD with poems read by the poets)

Hip Hop Speaks to Children selected by Nikki Giovanni (includes a CD)

When Did You Last Wash Your Feet? by Michael Rosen

No Breathing in Class by Michael Rosen

Postcards

This project can be done for any occasion, but Father's Day works well.

Grades K–8

Subjects Language Arts, Media Studies, Math

Time Frame Two or three lessons

Materials White Bristol board, rulers, pencils, colored pencils, scissors

Bring in samples of postcards from various places around the world, if possible. Share with the class the history of postcards (patented in 1861 and originally intended to provide a lower cost way to send a short message). Talk to the class about how postcards were a popular way for people to communicate during vacations in the years before email and easy phone access. Discuss the typical size (approximately 4 by 6 inches / 10 by 15 cm), the division of the back into message and address sections, and the fact that it is unnecessary to put a postcard in an envelope.

Have students do a rough copy of their own postcard on plain paper to ensure their measurements are correct and so that they can practice the spacing of their words.

Students will then measure and cut a postcard out of white Bristol board, draw a picture on the front, write a message, and address the postcard.

For younger students, provide them with a precut postcard. Some will require an adult to print the address legibly, but they can write or copy a short message on their own and draw their own picture.

Students can bring in a stamp from home (perhaps your school will cover the expense for students who are unable to bring one). When postcards are finished, walk as a class to a mailbox close to the school and mail the postcards a week or so in advance of Father's Day. Students with non-traditional families can send their postcard to any special person in their life. Be sure to remind your young students that it's a secret!

Book Tie-ins

Mail Myself to You
  by Woody Guthrie
(see notes on Woody Guthrie
  with Flat Stanley project)

The Principal's New Clothes

All kids will love designing outfits for your school's principal or some other good sport volunteer.

Grades K–8

Subjects Language Arts, Art

Time Frame One or two lessons to read and discuss the stories, two or more lessons for outfit design and drawing, one session to share student work

Materials Photo of the face of your volunteer good sport grownup, sized to a height of between 1 and 1½ inches and color photocopied so that each child has one (plus some for extras); background paper for mounting the drawings, coloring materials and glue

Find a good sport grownup in your school who would be willing to have his or her face on student-designed outfits. It could be you, your principal, teacher-librarian or any other staff member. Be sure to get the permission of your good sport volunteer first!

Share the book *The Principal's New Clothes* with the class. See if the students make the connection to the classic *The Emperor's New Clothes.* Read that story to them as well.

Get the children thinking about outfitting the good sport grownup who has volunteered to be a part of this activity. Set the children to work designing an outfit for that person. Have them do a rough sketch, then a good

Seasonal Projects

Most of the projects in this book can be done at any time of year, but the ones listed below are well suited for specific seasons.

Fall
First Day of School
   Questionnaire*
Leaf Pictures
Leaf Project
Pumpkin Study
Reading Survey
Shoes

Winter
Amaryllis Plant
Friendship Hearts
Hibernation Day
Winter Garden

Spring/Summer
Birds
Butterfly Life Cycle in Pasta
Desert Island Adventure
Earth Day Globes
It Looked Like Spilt Milk
Last Day of School
   Questionnaire (see *)
Planet Walk

copy that will be carefully detailed and colored in. Glue the photo of the head onto the display paper with the outfit. Be sure to display these in a high-traffic area of the school, as they will be a big hit!

You may need to have a word with your students about what type and style of clothing design is appropriate for the purposes of this assignment.

For younger grades, children can follow the same format or cut pieces of clothing out of magazines or catalogs and glue onto a paper to form an outfit. Top with the head photo.

Note: There is a way to print out a sheet with multiple photos in the size you need. If you do not know how to make one, speak to the resident computer expert in your school or family to save time and extra work.

Book Tie-ins

The Principal's New Clothes
   by Stephanie Calmenson

The Emperor's New Clothes
   by Hans Christian Andersen
   (available with illustrations
   by many different people,
   notably Virginia Lee Burton,
   Alison Jay and Demi)

Guests in the Classroom

Make the most of your school staff! Most principals and vice principals are happy to be visited by students with a story to read or a piece of work to show. Have specialty teachers, school secretaries and custodians come in and read their favorite story to your class. With younger students, use your shared writing time to write chart paper letters to staff members. Include a piece of chart paper for them to respond, and use the response for shared reading.

If you have a staff member who has a talent, collection or special interest that is appropriate to your grade level, you could invite them in to do a presentation, a Q & A, or a 20 Questions style session where your students try to guess what the guest's specialty is.

Spread the net wider and tap your friends to visit your classroom. A friend of mine was a jewelry store owner, and did a presentation about birthstones for my class as they were studying rocks and minerals. He brought a sample of each type of stone and the kids were mesmerized! The friend in question later left the world of jewelry and became a teacher, so who inspired who?

Pumpkin Study

As the fall weather moves in and Thanksgiving approaches many classes study the changing leaves and harvest time. Studying the inside and outside of a pumpkin can cover many curriculum areas and concepts.

Grades K–6

Subjects Science, Language Arts, Art, Math

Time Frame Three to five lessons

Materials One pumpkin for a whole class lesson or one pumpkin per group for middle grade independent investigation. Additional materials for each individual activity are listed below

Estimating the circumference of the pumpkin

Materials String, scissors, sticky note flags, chart paper

By looking at the pumpkin, each student will estimate how much string it will take to wrap around the middle of the middle of the pumpkin exactly.

Younger students will come to you individually, show you the length of string they think will be right, and you will cut the string and give it to the child with a sticky note flag around the end labeled with the child's name.

Middle grade students can cut the length of string they feel is right and attach a labeled sticky note flag.

Gather the class together and have each child in turn wrap their string around the pumpkin. Have a chart (on the board or on chart paper) set up with the headings Too Long, Just Right, Too Short. Have each child check their string in relation to the pumpkin, and then tape the string onto the graph under the appropriate heading. Discuss the results.

Middle grade students can then calculate the exact circumference of the pumpkin, measure their string and calculate how close they were to the correct answer.

Looking inside the pumpkin

Materials The seeds from a pumpkin you have been studying (they need to be washed and laid out on newspaper to dry the day before the activity)

Have each child guess the number of seeds that were in the pumpkin.

Record answers on a chart. Have the students arrange the dried pumpkin seeds in groups of 10 (*older students* could do groups of 25). Count the groups of seeds to determine the total number of seeds in the pumpkin. Go back to the chart and have students determine if their guess was over or under the correct number. *Middle grade students* could calculate how much over or under they were.

Pumpkin seed art

Materials The seeds that were dried and counted in the pumpkin seed activity, orange construction paper, white paper, orange yarn or tempera paint (depending on grade level), Bristol board (for middle grades)

Do this activity after students have had the opportunity to look inside a pumpkin.

For younger students, precut orange construction paper into the shape of a pumpkin for each child. Also precut white paper into the shape of a pumpkin (slightly smaller than the orange one). Some students may be able to cut their own pumpkin shapes if lines are drawn on the paper to guide them. They will glue the white paper onto the orange one, and glue pumpkin seeds and orange yarn (in a squiggle shape) onto the white paper to make it look like the "guts" of the pumpkin.

For middle grade students, have them create a mosaic picture, concrete or abstract, using painted pumpkin seeds. A couple of days before the activity, put batches of dried pumpkin seeds into a shallow dish, squirt some tempera paint on them, mix them around and put them on newspaper to dry overnight. Do several batches with different colors. Students will sketch a picture on Bristol board using large shapes (easier to fill in), then glue on seeds to create the effect and colors they want. A lesson on mosaic technique and famous mosaic art goes well with this project.

Pumpkin statistics

Materials Measuring tape, scale, recording sheet

Students will count the number of lines on the pumpkin and measure its height and weight.

For younger students, count the lines as a class while the teacher points to each one, and measure the height and weight as a group.

   Middle grade students can carry out their investigations in small groups using one pumpkin per group.

Sink or float

Materials Large container, water

Have each student predict whether the pumpkin will sink or float. Record the predictions. Do the activity as a class *for younger students. Middle grade students* can do the recording of the predictions and results in the same group they had for pumpkin statistics.

Book Tie-ins

Pumpkin Circle: The Story of a Garden by George Levenson

It's a Fruit, It's a Vegetable, It's a Pumpkin by Allan Fowler

It's Pumpkin Time by Zoe Hall

Pumpkin, Pumpkin by Jeanne Titherington

The Pumpkin Patch by Elizabeth King

Growing a pumpkin seed

Materials Zip lock bags, potting soil, one pumpkin seed per student

Students will plant a pumpkin seed in a zip lock bag. Label each bag with a child's name before you begin. Put some dirt and a small amount of water in the bag and add a pumpkin seed. Make a few extra bags in case some seeds do not sprout. Zip up the bags and place them on a table where students can see them.

In a few days the students will be able to observe the bags fogging up and clearing, and they will see the seeds opening up, roots reaching down, and a sprout growing up. When the seeds sprout, send the bags home with a note giving instructions on replanting in a pot.

Additional pumpkin activities

For younger students:
- Make pumpkin-scented play dough. Use the recipe in the Play Dough Predictor project (page 86), but add one container of pumpkin pie spice (1½ oz./approx. 42 g). Put some small foil pie and muffin tins with the play dough so students can make pumpkin "pies." Remind them that although it smells good enough to eat, don't eat it!
- Start with a photocopied outline of a pumpkin. Have children tear small pieces of orange construction or tissue paper and glue it inside the pumpkin shape. Use green for the stem. Do a quick lesson on careful, controlled tearing before you begin.

For middle grade students:
- Using the letters p, u, m, n, k and i, challenge the students to put the letters together to make 12 words. Letters can be used more than once. (Answers: ink, kin nip, pin, pip, pun, pup, punk, pink, mink, pump, pumpkin)
- Think of creative uses for pumpkins (for example, Cinderella's pumpkin was used as a coach). Write and illustrate the idea, either individually or in small groups.

One-Day Projects

Sometimes you're looking for something a little different. A morale-booster for you and your students, something that's quick, easy and fun, and a valuable learning experience in the process. These projects can all be done in just one day.

Alphabet Adventure
Butterfly Life Cycle
Circles
Computer-Made Graphic Organizer
Extra Fun Day
First Day of School Questionnaire
Folded Paper Art
Fruit or Vegetable Drawing
Hibernation Day
It Looked Like Spilt Milk

Math Olympics
Page One
Planet Walk
Play Money Spelling Bee
Poetry Circle
Precise Communication
Reading Survey
Read Posters
Report To Mission Control
Rock Review
Self-Evaluation
Shoes
Simulated Space Walk
Six Word Memoirs
Speed Of Light
Ten Apples Up On Top
Trading Card
Trivia Quiz
Understanding Craters

Reading Awards

Involve your students in a larger reading community through a local reading awards program.

Grades K–8

Subjects Language Arts

Time Frame Varies depending on the program; students usually read books over a period of a few months

Materials The program sponsor will provide you with information

Look into reading programs in your area in which students can participate.

For example, the Ontario Library Association sponsors the Forest of Reading program, which provides children at various age levels the opportunity to read nominated books and vote for the one they like the best. This project can be taken on by a class, an interest group or even the whole school. Students set up voting lists and polling booths, thus learning about the voting process (which mirrors provincial voting guidelines). There are lists of books for all grade levels. In the Forest of Reading program, awards are presented in a ceremony each May, and students are invited to attend. At the ceremony they have the opportunity to meet the authors, buy and get

A (very small) sampling of picture books for upper grade students:

The works of Chris Van Allsburg

The works of Ian Wallace

The Wall by Peter Sis

Tibet: Through the Red Box by Peter Sis

Math Curse by Jon Scieszka

Science Verse by Jon Scieszka

The Wonderful Towers of Watts by Patricia Zelver

The Edmund Fitzgerald by Kathy-Jo Wargin

The Three Astronauts by Umberto Eco

The Bomb and the General by Umberto Eco

All Those Secrets of the World by Jane Yolen

In Flanders Fields by Linda Granfield

Galimoto by Karen Lynn Williams

The Way to Start a Day by Byrd Baylor

Five Secrets in a Box by Catherine Brighton

The Kid Line by Teddy Jam

Martin's Big Words by Doreen Rappaport

Be Boy Buzz by Bell Hooks

Cookies: Bite-Size Life Lessons by Amy Krouse Rosenthal

The Man Who Walked Between the Towers by Mordecai Gerstein

Mr. Maxwell's Mouse by Frank Asch

Tulips by Jay O'Callahan

The Incredible Painting of Felix Clousseau by Jon Agee

Once Upon a Time, The End (Asleep in 60 Seconds) by Geoffrey Kloske

Cinder Edna by Ellen Jackson

Faithful Elephants by Yukio Tsuchiya

Rose Blanche by Roberto Innocenti

The Necklace by Guy de Maupassant, illustrated by Gary Kelley

The pop-up books of Robert Sabuda and David A. Carter

Using Picture Books with Older Students

Teachers of young children routinely read aloud and share picture books with their students many times each day. As the students mature and move up the grade levels, many teachers sharply reduce the amount of read-aloud time and stop sharing picture books altogether.

Adolescents are growing up, but are at heart "little kids in big bodies" and still enjoy being read to. Sharing selections from books that you are reading yourself, giving book talks to promote materials new to the school or classroom, and exposing the students to wide ranges of literature, sometimes just for fun, are ways you can keep older students as closely connected to books as their younger counterparts.

Involve your teacher-librarian in the literary life of your classroom too. Ask at your public library if a librarian would be willing to come to your school to give guest book talks to your students or arrange a class trip to the public library.

Don't be limited by the age recommendation on a picture book. Many of them, though targeted at and appropriate for young children, contain subtleties, humor, complexities and subtext that can only be appreciated by an older and more sophisticated mind. Older children often return to previously viewed TV shows or films and take away new understanding, and the same holds true for picture books.

In fact, there are many picture books that are very much above the comprehension level of young children and deal with subject matter that makes them uninteresting to and actually unsuitable for them. These are the books to seek out for use with upper elementary students.

The challenge for teachers of upper elementary grades is to introduce picture books to their students as a complement to nonfiction texts and novels and to teach the power and beauty that picture books can contain. Easy-to-read books can be used as an introduction to a topic and a way to focus attention on the basics of a subject. In addition, visual learners, ESL students or students who do best at a lower reading level can benefit from the presence of picture books in a class collection.

When planning units and lessons for your classroom, add a new dimension to learning by consulting with your school's teacher-librarian or a public librarian to get recommendations for picture books that will enhance your program. Or take the plunge and go to your public library for a few hours after school or on a weekend, and immerse yourself in the richness and diversity of the world of picture books.

books autographed, and share in the excitement of the moment the winner is declared.

The Texas Library Association sponsors the Bluebonnet Awards. California has the Young Reader Medal Program. Florida has the Sunshine State Young Readers. Iowa has the Children's Choice Award. The oldest children's choice award in the U.S. and Canada is the Pacific Northwest Library Association's Young Reader's Choice Award, established in 1940. It is the only regional award chosen by children of two countries.

Check with your teacher-librarian, your local public librarian or a library association in your area for information about a reading program near you.

Giving a Book Talk

When sharing picture books (or novels) with older students, it's all in the prefacing. Grab them with a detail. Frame the story for them. Give them a background, a point of reference, something to look for in the story. Read the first few pages or a short excerpt from the book. Show a couple of the illustrations and discuss the style. Talk about the author. Intricate pop-up books are great attention-grabbers.

Reading Survey

This is a good way to kick off your year in reading. Students will answer six questions about their reading preferences, then compare their answers with other students.

Grades 4–8

Subjects Language Arts

Time Frame One session, approximately 45 minutes to an hour

Materials Photocopied reading survey for each student, separate paper for recording stapled to the survey

Give the students a short, six-question reading survey to complete on their own. See the template on the next page. Staple a separate blank piece of paper to the survey on which students record their findings when they compare their answers with those of their classmates. After a 10-minute quiet time to complete and think about the survey by themselves, give students time to move around the classroom stopping to compare answers with classmates.

To record information, students write the name of the student they are talking to and the number of questions they got the same answer for: for example, Christian 2, Monica 0, Andrew 4.

After students have had about 15 to 20 minutes to meet with various classmates (they will not have time to compare with every other student in the class), collect all the surveys and comparing sheets, and ask students to share with you what they are thinking about the activity.

Read each question to the class and ask them to answer by show of hands for each answer. Students can look around and see how many students answered as they did, and who felt differently. Segue into a discussion about reading preferences, types of literature that will be covered in class this year, and anything else you or the students wish to discuss.

The interactive nature of this activity provides:
- you a chance to establish guidelines the year for student interaction, acceptable noise level and on-task behavior,
- the students a chance to meet and talk with each other informally on a set topic and to get used to class guidelines while you observe and monitor their progress,
- an overview of the areas of interest in reading of your new students,
- a basis for forming either homogeneous or heterogeneous groupings of students based on their areas of literary interest.

Reading Survey

1. Would you rather read:
   a. the newspaper
   b. information from a website
   c. a magazine
   d. a fiction book
   e. a nonfiction book

2. Would you rather read:
   a. on or under the covers in bed
   b. in the public library
   c. on a park bench
   d. at your desk at school
   e. on your living room couch

3. If you were going to read a book to younger children, would you choose:
   a. *The Cat in the Hat*
   b. a Robert Munsch book
   c. Mother Goose rhymes
   d. *Curious George*
   e. *The Very Hungry Caterpillar*

4. What is your favorite type of fiction book?
   a. adventure
   b. historical fiction
   c. animal stories
   d. realistic
   e. fantasy

5. What is your favorite type of nonfiction book?
   a. biography
   b. history
   c. poetry
   d. sports
   e. science

6. Would you rather:
   a. read quietly to yourself
   b. read out loud
   c. have someone read to you
   d. listen to a recorded reading
   e. read to someone else

Reading Time

Give students a variety of opportunities so they look forward to independent reading time.

Grades K–8

Subjects Language Arts

Time Frame A portion of each school day (time depends on grade level)

Materials Lots of books

Most classrooms have an independent reading time each day, where students are reading self-selected books. Give some variety to the program by introducing some of the following ideas on various "special" reading days. Special reading days could be scheduled once a month or more frequently, depending on your class. Students will look forward to those days and begin to plan ahead what reading material they will bring to school.

Here are some variations on independent reading time:

- "read anything you want" day, when students may bring hockey or baseball cards, comic books, magazines, etc.
- quiet reading (each student reads his/her own book, no talking or sharing)
- "unquiet" reading day, where students may share a book with a partner or small group and talk quietly while they read
- "bring a book from home" day for classes where students usually read classroom/school books
- "reading activity" day, when students can work on word search, crossword, or other word puzzles instead of reading a book

After independent reading time, have a group share time when students can share what they have read or ask questions (see Group Share After Reading at pages 60–61).

READ Posters

Take a photo of each student and then create and print out individual READ posters.

Grades K–8

Subjects Language Arts

Time Frame Time for teacher to take a photo of each child and follow software directions to print out a poster

Materials Digital camera, paper for printer

The American Library Association (ALA) has software that allows you to print out individual READ posters using a child's photo. The completed poster can be used as a motivator for reading, as a reward for a job well done or as a gift to each child.

Talk to your teacher-librarian about acquiring the CDs and putting them to use in your school. The ALA also has a great selection of reading posters and bookmarks for your classroom or school library. Check out the ALA store at www.alastore.ala.org.

Professional Reading

Check out these touchstone texts to inspire your teaching of reading and writing:

Lasting Impressions by Shelley Harwayne

In the Middle by Nancie Atwell

The Art of Teaching Reading by Lucy McCormick Calkins

The Art of Teaching Writing by Lucy McCormick Calkins

Radical Reflections by Mem Fox

Reading Essentials by Regie Routman

The Reading Zone by Nancie Atwell

Even Hockey Players Read by David Booth

Kid Writing by Eileen Feldgus and Isabell Cardonick

Report to Mission Control

Just as astronauts need to be able to make clear, precise reports to Mission Control, children learn to be careful and exact in their descriptions.

Grades K–8

Subjects Language Arts

Time Frame One session

Materials A different candy bar for each group of three or four students, paper for recording answers

Note: Before doing this activity, ensure that there are no allergy concerns!

Astronauts undergo rigorous training in many areas, including communication. They need to be able to report to Mission Control and to each other in precise language that leaves no room for misinterpretation or ambiguity. This exercise helps students to focus their attention on careful word selection and exact description. They will conduct a discovery and write up a report being as exact as possible in their communication.

As a class, discuss the need for astronauts to be able to communicate in very precise language, whether describing something they see or explaining a problem.

The class will then hone their communication skills while working in small groups of three or four students. Each group will be given a candy bar to examine and then describe, being as precise as possible.

Cut the candy bar in half so that students may describe both the outside and the inside. Each group will be given a piece of chart paper entitled "Report to Mission Control." They will come up with and record a list of words to describe their candy bar.

For younger students, the teacher can work with one group at a time to create the list of

describing words and scribe for the students or supervise their writing.

Middle and upper grade groups can create their own chart, which can be divided into sections such as Taste, Texture, Ingredients, etc.

Book Tie-ins

Don't Forget the Bacon by Pat Hutchins

Vision for Space by Joe Lennox (this book is a memoir that describes how the author's life has been connected to the space program. An interesting read for adults, lots of excerpts to read aloud to kids).

The ABCs of Space Exploration by Joe Lennox

Then have someone who was not in the classroom during the lesson come in as a guest to hear the lists and determine which chocolate bar is being described. Your guest could be the school principal, a parent volunteer, a specialty teacher (French, Phys. Ed.) or other school personnel.

Each group will read their list of words while the guest looks at all the chocolate bars, which have been set up on a table. The guest will try to determine which chocolate bar the group is describing.

After all the lists have been read and the guessing and revealing are done, you can cut the bars into pieces (you may need a few extras) and enjoy a class treat!

Rock Review

To teach or review the three types of rocks, bake these recipes, compare and contrast the look of each one and how it relates to the type of rock it represents.

Grades 3–8

Subjects Science, Language Arts, Math, Art

Time Frame One lesson, 1 hour-plus for baking (or three individual baking lessons, depending how you choose to format the class), and one or two class lessons following

Materials

For Cereal Balls (igneous rock): $\frac{1}{3}$ cup margarine, 10 oz. bag of marshmallows, $6\frac{1}{2}$ cups crispy rice cereal, waxed paper for finished treats

For Layer Bars (sedimentary rock): $\frac{1}{2}$ cup margarine, $1\frac{1}{2}$ cups graham cracker crumbs, 1 can sweetened condensed milk, 1 cup chocolate chips, $1\frac{1}{3}$ cups shredded coconut, 9-by-13-inch baking pan

For Two-Chocolate Bark (metamorphic rock): 12 oz. white chocolate chips, 12 oz. regular chocolate chips, 2 microwaveable bowls, 9-by-13-inch baking pan, waxed paper to line pan

Book Tie-ins

If You Find a Rock by Peggy Christian
Rocks and Minerals by DK Publishing
Everybody Needs a Rock by Byrd Baylor
The Pebble in My Pocket by Meredith Hooper
Looking at Rocks (My First Field Guides) by Jennifer Dussling

Note: Before doing this activity, ensure that there are no allergy concerns!

The class could be divided into three groups for the making of the recipes, one for each recipe (perhaps with a parent volunteer supervising), and each group could present their finished product to the rest of the class.

Igneous Rock: Cereal Balls

Air is trapped in the cereal much like air gets trapped in pumice when molten rock cools quickly.

Melt $\frac{1}{3}$ cup margarine with a 10 oz. package of marshmallows in a medium to large pot. Remove from heat. Stir in $6\frac{1}{2}$ cups of crispy rice cereal. Form the mixture into balls and cool on waxed paper.

Sedimentary Rock: Layer Bars

Each ingredient represents a different layer of sediment.

Preheat the oven to 350° F. In a 9-by-13-inch pan, melt ½ cup of margarine. Sprinkle 1½ cups graham cracker crumbs over the margarine. Pour one can sweetened condensed milk evenly over the crumbs. Top with 1 cup chocolate chips, 1⅓ cups coconut. Press down firmly. Bake for 25 to 30 minutes. Cut into bars when cooled.

Metamorphic Rock: Two-Chocolate Bark

The swirling white and dark chocolate resembles marble, a metamorphic rock.

Place 12 oz. of white chocolate and 12 oz. of chocolate chips in separate bowls. Melt each in the microwave for 2 to 3 minutes, stopping midway to stir. Pour the melted white chocolate into the dark. Stir lightly to swirl, not mix. Pour the swirled mixture into a pan lined with waxed paper, then refrigerate till hardened. Break the treat into pieces to share with the class.

When the three recipes are made (same day or the next day, depending on your schedule), distribute a piece of each to every member of the class. Before anyone eats, have the students study the three samples.

Possibilities for recording the similarities between each treat and the category of rock it represents are:
• working as a group to create a class chart
• students recording information in small groups
• students working individually

For younger students, provide a template for recording information. Students of all ages could also draw sketches of each of the treats.

Enjoy eating the treats when the work is done.

Mixed-Grade Projects

These projects provide an opportunity for teachers and students to work together across grade levels. Fostering interaction between students of different ages builds a stronger school community as well as learning opportunities for both younger and older students. And it's fun!

Books for Younger Students

Brown Paper Characters

Extra Fun Day

Pumpkin Study

School Multicultural Project

Stop, Drop and Read Day

Student Books Modeled on a Published Book

Sugar Cube Creations

School Multicultural Project

This is a whole school project that can involve students or entire families. Each class will study a country, its culture, customs and food, and mount a display of their findings, and each student will have a passport to visit all the other "countries."

Grades K–8

Subjects Social Studies, Language Arts, Art

Time Frame Several weeks preparation, one day celebration

Materials Books and other research materials about chosen country

Each class in the school studies a different country/culture (countries can be chosen at a staff meeting).

The class will learn about the people, culture, and customs of the chosen country and plan a classroom display of their findings (including map, flag, money if possible, food, and music if possible).

While your class is researching and preparing the classroom display, use a video camera to capture all the activity and play it back as people are visiting the classroom. Another approach is to videotape each child giving one fact about the country you are studying, and have the tape running in the background during the visiting time. *Upper grade students* could prepare a Power Point presentation that would repeat throughout the day or evening.

If you choose to include food as a part of the project, be sure to take the usual precautions to address allergy concerns.

On the presentation day, classes will rotate around the school to the decorated and set-up classrooms. Half the class will remain in the classroom to answer questions and display the materials, other half will visit other classrooms, and then they switch places.

Rotations are coordinated by school-wide announcements that signal to students when to move to the next class. Teachers have a schedule and route map.

Teachers will design a paper "passport," which each student will carry and have stamped as students visit each class/country. Teachers will arrange for a stamp or sticker to represent the chosen country for each class.

Involve the families of your students by having the event take place during Open House or Education Week. Meet the Creature (the first parent-teacher night) is typically too early to pull off this kind of extravaganza.

More Ideas for School Multicultural Projects

- Ask parents or people from the local community to come in to display and talk about traditional cultural clothing.

- Include an arts and crafts component so students can try origami, henna patterns, using chopsticks, etc.

- Read traditional stories from various countries.

- Traditional dances could be showcased and taught to students.

Book Tie-ins

Whoever You Are by Mem Fox

All the Colors of the Earth by Sheila Hamanaka

If the World Were a Village by David Smith and Shelagh Armstrong

Material World: A Global Family Portrait by Peter Menzel

The Richard and Robert Sherman song "It's a Small World" fits well with this project.

Self-Evaluation

Students will fill in a blank report card form—for themselves!

Grades 3–8

Time Frame One session for set-up and explanation, one session for filling in the form, possible individual conferencing afterwards

Materials Copies of a blank report card form

This activity provides students with a chance to develop their self-assessment skills and teachers with an interesting insight into how their students see and evaluate themselves and their work.

A few days before report cards go home, give each student a blank copy of the actual report card they will receive. Go over it with them and explain the categories and what each one means. Have them fill in the form with the marks and comments they would give themselves. Collect the forms.

After the official report cards are sent home and students have had a chance to look at them, schedule a short interview time with each student. Discuss strengths, areas for improvement and next steps.

Look at the student-written report card as well, and ask and answer any questions that arise.

You will be surprised how accurate, insightful and hard on themselves your students are!

Assessment, Evaluation and Reporting

Each school board and district has its own guidelines for assessment, evaluation, and reporting. The criteria, descriptors, qualifiers and actual reporting systems vary by state, province and country. To assess and evaluate your students' achievement when using the projects in this book, teachers should refer to the accepted practices of their own school system.

It is an expectation of school systems that assessment involve diagnostic, formative and summative assessment information. The methods and tools used most often include pencil and paper (formal testing), performance assessments (projects, presentations) and personal communication (conferences, journals). Most areas also involve the students in self-assessment.

Rubrics are frequently used to assess student achievement and communicate student achievement to parents. Many school boards have published exemplars for teachers to use for assessment. These illustrate for parents and students the expected level of achievement.

As with all curriculum delivered to students, teachers will need to use strategies to accommodate and or modify for English language learners, special needs students and students with an IEP.

Familiarity with local assessment, evaluation and reporting expectations will allow teachers to choose the most appropriate way to assess the progress and performance of their own students as they participate in the projects in this book.

Book Tie-ins

The Bad-News Report Card
 by Nancy Poydar
The Report Card
 by Andrew Clements

Web Help

The parent-teacher interview is a great time to form a partnership with parents in the education of their child. Here are some useful websites to help you prepare for interviews:

www.priceless-teaching-strategies.com/
 parent_teacher_communication.html

www.canadianliving.com/family/parenting/
 ask_an_expert improving_parent_teacher_
 interviews.php

The following website provides interview tips for parents in twelve different languages:

www.peopleforeducation.com/parent-teacher

Shoes

*Students have fun working in groups to gather information
and construct graphs using data about their shoes.*

Grades 3–8

Subjects Math

Time Frame One lesson for gathering information, two to four lessons to collate information and construct graphs, one or two lessons to present information and discuss

Materials Copy of the class list for each student, paper, rulers and coloring materials for graph construction

This is a fun small-group and yet whole class activity. It is a good icebreaker for the first couple of weeks of school, as it gets the students interacting with each other socially and working together on a project. This activity is best done after a quick review of how to make a tally chart, and different types of graphs.

Divide the students into groups of no more than three or four (or let them self-select their group). Tell the students they will be gathering information about each other's shoes.

Assign each group a topic on which they will survey the class and record information. Some topics are suited to stronger students, as they will have a lot of information to collate: for example, store and size. Other topics, such as open or closed toe, will be easier to handle for students who are not as strong. Suggested topics include size, color, symbol, store where the shoes were purchased, brand name, open or closed toe, type of shoe (running shoe, sandal, dress shoe), store where the shoes were bought, etc.

Give each group 10 to 15 minutes to plan a strategy and talk about their task, then groups will circulate around the class gathering and recording information. Groups will check in with the teacher after each stage of the project to show their rough work, have it checked, and receive approval to move on.

After groups have gathered their information, they will meet again to collate their findings. Initial collation should be on the back of the information sheet, and should take the form of a tally chart.

The next step is to talk as a group about construction of the graph, and to construct a rough copy graph. Tailor the type of graph for each grade level and group to their ability level and curriculum requirements. For example, *younger students* could create a simple picture or bar graph using a photocopied template; *upper grade students* could handle line or circle graphs as well and possibly create their own template.

Book Tie-ins

On Your Feet
  by Karin Luisa Badt
What Can You Do With a Shoe?
  by Beatrice Schenk de Regniers
Shoes Shoes Shoes by Ann Morris
Two Shoes, Blue Shoes, New Shoes
  by Sally Fitz-Gibbon

After the rough copy graph has been checked by the teacher, students will construct a good copy graph on graph chart paper (if available) or another large sheet of paper. Good copy graphs will be posted in the classroom and each group will present their findings to the class. When each group has presented, graphs can be posted in the school library or on the walls in the hallway for other classes to look at.

Simulated Space Walk

Who hasn't imagined being an astronaut and floating in space? This activity gives students the opportunity to experience in a small way the challenges of working in space.

Grades K–8

Subjects Science, Language Arts

Time Frame One lesson for the demonstration, one or two lessons for follow-up discussion and activities

Materials Two metal braces, a nut and a screw, a screwdriver and nut pliers, thick winter gloves (several sets allow more than one student to take a turn at the same time)

Most of us have dreamed about what it would be like to be weightless and to float in space. That's the fun part. When astronauts do their space walks, the purpose is usually to complete an important task related to their mission.

Talk with the class about astronauts and the tasks they perform while in space both inside and outside the spacecraft. Discuss EVA, Extra Vehicular Activity. The first spacewalk was done on March 18, 1965, by Soviet cosmonaut Alexei Leonov. American astronaut Ed White followed on June 3, 1965. These websites contain information and show labeled photos of space suits: www.hightechscience.org/eva_suit.htm; www.spaceflight.nasa.gov/station/eva/spacesuit.html.

During EVA, astronauts do repairs on the spacecraft, capture, repair and deploy satellites, service and make improvements to the Hubble Telescope and test new equipment for spacewalking. This all takes place over 200 miles above the surface of the Earth while traveling at over 17,000 miles per hour.

Brainstorm the things a spacesuit must do in order to keep an astronaut safe outside the spaceship (for example, provide oxygen and proper pressure, maintain appropriate

temperature, contain a communication system, tether the astronaut safely to the spacecraft, allow for mobility, shield against ultraviolet radiation). With the adaptations of the space suit, there are also disadvantages.

Have students work in pairs to attach the two metal braces together with a nut and a screw. Time each student to see how many seconds it takes.

Tell the students they will be performing the task again, but this time they will try to simulate (in a small way) the conditions an astronaut would face in space-walk conditions. After placing the nut, the screw and the tools back in their starting position, students will then put on a pair of heavy winter gloves and attempt to attach the screw and the nut to the braces again.

This time, the challenge begins with just picking up the items to be used for the job. Students will learn that the task will require strict concentration, and the more precise they can be in communicating with each other, the easier the task will become.

After students have had a chance to try fastening the braces together, talk in small or large groups about the following space challenges and how NASA accommodates for them.

- Astronauts need to communicate with each other. (There is a radio system within the helmet.)
- Tools could easily float away. (They are tethered to the wrists of the spacesuit.)
- It is difficult to move fingers in large gloves. (Use specially designed tools, use power tools to complete jobs faster.)

- There is less gravity in space—astronauts would drift away from the job. (There are footholds to lock into, astronauts use the space arm to carry them to where they need to be, there are a series of handgrips to help them move around.)
- The spacecraft will enter darkness every 45 minutes as the spacecraft orbits the Earth and passes through day and night. (Lights on the helmet to illuminate the task.)

One way to accomplish the discussion is to post chart paper around the room, each with one of the challenges on it. Divide the class into the same number of groups as you have charts, and have groups rotate around to each chart and write their solutions/ideas, moving along at time intervals set by you (five minutes or so). At the end, read and discuss all the ideas on each chart together.

This project can be simplified to its basic facts for use *with younger students*. For example, show a picture of astronauts doing a space walk and then have students try such tasks as stacking building blocks, a baby's plastic ring stacking set or a child's shape sorting toy. Additional details can be added to suit the grade level of your students.

Book Tie-ins

Space Walks (Our Solar System) by Dana Meachen Rau and Nadia Higgins

DK Readers: Astronaut, Living in Space by Kate Hayden

How Do You Go to the Bathroom in Space? by William R. Pogue

Six-Word Memoirs

Students will write an extremely compact story or description using only six words.

Grades 4–8

Subjects Language Arts

Time Frame Three to five lessons

Materials Examples of six-word stories

The story goes that Ernest Hemingway once won a ten-dollar bet by writing a complete story in six words. The words? "For sale: baby shoes, never worn."

We often try to get students to extend their writing by adding descriptive passages and more details. In this exercise, students learn the opposite: about economy of words, writing in a set format and making every word count.

Smith magazine is an online home for storytelling, with a focus on personal narrative. They believe everyone has a story, and everyone should have a place to tell it. Smith has challenged its readers to come up with a six-word memoir. In 2008 they published a book, *Not Quite What I Was Planning,* a collection of six-word memoirs by writers famous and obscure. Have students try this. Talk about the notion of saying a lot in just a few words. Read them examples that are age appropriate from the book or from this website, which also contains an example of a book put together by third grade students, www.smithmag.net/sixwords/.

Some examples:
Five continents down, two to go.
Age 11: became a middle child.
Fourteen years old, story still untold.
Should have learned to count.
Looking to know everything about everything

Warmups for this activity can be done as a class, in small groups or individually.
- Use spelling list words, such as "Use three spelling words in an eight-word sentence." Practice with different numbers of spelling words and words in the sentence.
- Pick a topic and brainstorm a list of the six most descriptive words on that topic.

Book Tie-ins

(books that tell a story with few words)

Blue Hat, Green Hat by Sandra Boynton
Yo! Yes? by Chris Raschka
Not Quite What I Was Planning: Six-Word Memoirs by Writers Famous and Obscure ed. Rachel Fershleiser and Larry Smith

No-Word Memoirs

From six words, you could make the leap to no words. An adjunct to this project could be a study of wordless books, telling a story with pictures only.

Deep in the Forest by Brinton Turkle

Carl's Christmas by Alexandra Day (there is a series of Carl books)

Dinosaur Dream by Dennis Nolan (dream sequence is wordless)

Snow Day by Daniel Peddle

Free Fall by David Wiesner

Smashed Potatoes

Students write out the recipe (ingredients, then directions) for their favorite food. Recipes are collected and bound into a book.

Grades K–3

Subjects Language Arts

Time Frame One introductory lesson to talk about cooking, baking, favorite foods and recipes, one or two lessons to write the ingredients and directions, one lesson to draw the pictures

Materials Paper, coloring materials, book binding materials

An oldie, and yet fresh and hilarious with each new group of children. This is a great Mother's Day gift!

Begin by talking about cooking, baking, favorite foods and recipes. Have some cookbooks on hand so that students may see the format. Have the children think of their favorite food, a food they think they know how to make or a food they have watched someone prepare.

Children write out the recipe (ingredients, then directions) for their chosen food. They draw a picture to go with the recipe, and each student's work is collected and compiled into a class book that can be photocopied and bound. Kindergarten students can dictate their recipe to the teacher or a class volunteer who will type up and print out a copy that can be illustrated by the student, then photocopied and bound.

The books make great gifts for Mother's Day or other occasions.

Book Tie-ins

Smashed Potatoes edited by Jane G. Martell (this book is difficult to find as it was published in 1974)

Pete's a Pizza by William Steig

Cooking Rocks! Rachael Ray 30-Minute Meals for Kids by Rachael Ray

Never Take a Pig to Lunch by Nadine Bernard Westcott (this book is also difficult to find)

D.W. the Picky Eater by Marc Brown

For books that are out of print or difficult to find, check out used book stores in your area or online booksellers such as Alibris, or the used book feature at Amazon.com or Barnes and Noble.com. It's worth the effort to track down some of these timeless gems.

Snail Terrarium

Set up a snail terrarium in the classroom and use it as a focus for various class activities.

Grades K–3

Subjects Science, Math, Language Arts, Art

Time Frame Two or three weeks

Materials One or two clear terrariums with covers, paper towels, several live snails collected by you, spray bottle of water, a couple of pieces of chalk, small pieces of fruit and vegetables and or leaves, booklet for students to fill in, construction paper for art activity

Setting up a snail terrarium in your class works well at the beginning of the year as it provides a focal point of interest for your new students.

Snails are most active on a warm summer night, after a rainfall. They are sometimes found in the open, but can often be spotted around the edges of or under a rock or under flower pots and planters. Find the snails and have your snail terrariums up and running when the children come into the classroom.

Prepare the terrariums by placing moist paper towels on the floor and spraying the interior with water. Put in a few small pieces of fruit or vegetables and or leaves for food. Place pieces of chalk in each habitat to provide calcium, which snails need for shell growth and repair.

Secure the lid so the snails do not escape. Spray the walls of the habitat with water two or three times a week. Clean the habitat once or twice a week. Gently remove the snails by sliding them off the walls of the terrarium. If they look messy, rinse them quickly under cool water. Spray the walls of the habitat and wipe them clean with paper towels. If you are using paper on the floor of the habitat, replace it with new paper towels.

Book Tie-ins

Are You a Snail? by Judy Allen

A Snail's Pace (Rookie Read-About Science) by Allen Fowler

Slugs and Snails by Claire Llewellyn

Tiny Snail by Tammy Carter Bronson

The Snail's Spell by Joanne Ryder

A booklet can be made for students to work on. Pages include:

- A drawing by the student: "This is what my snail looks like."
- Labeled diagram of body parts (feelers, eyes, mouth, foot, slime, shell). Provide the drawing and have students print in the labels.
- A labeled diagram of the terrarium (air, plants, water, chalk, soil).
- A page to go home called "Science Homework for Mom and or Dad." Ask the parent to draw a picture of a snail (provide a paper with a box outlined for the drawing), and write a scientific fact to share with the child.

Class activities are based on science with a bit of measurement to see how long the slime trails are. The students have to estimate and then measure the slime trail using non-standard units such as plastic stacking cubes. Students can also incorporate obstacle courses made from building blocks to see if the snails can climb over the blocks.

No snails are harmed in the course of this project!

Snails in Art

A good art activity to accompany this study of snails is to examine and then emulate the famous collage by Henri Matisse called "The Snail." Print out a copy of "The Snail" or find a copy in a book to show the class. The Tate Museum in London has an excellent animated demonstration about this work at www.tate.org.uk/imap/pages/animated/cutout/matisse/snail.htm

Direct the children to follow the colors with their eyes, beginning with the green in the top right corner. Notice how the shapes form a spiral, snail-like design. Give the students a piece of construction paper to use as a background, and provide them with squares of construction paper in different colors, as well as glue. Children will first place, then glue down squares to form a snail shape. For younger students, draw a large spiral lightly in pencil on their background paper as a guide.

Speed of Light

Young children are excited to learn that they can keep counting and counting forever and they will not run out of numbers to count.

Grades 3–8

Subjects Math, Science

Time Frame One lesson for lead-up and preparation, one lesson for the activity, possible follow-up lessons

Materials Map of solar system, calculators

Children are fascinated by numbers that run into the millions, billions, or trillions and beyond. This activity allows students to work with very large numbers to figure out a concrete puzzle — how far does light travel in a year?

Begin with a class discussion on how light travels. Once it is established that light travels at a speed of 186,000 miles per second, challenge the students to come up with the distance light travels in one year.

The formula is: 186,000 x 60 (for distance in one minute), multiply that answer times 60 (for distance in one hour), multiply that answer times 24 (for distance in one day), multiply that answer times 365 for distance in one year.

Your answer should be in the neighborhood of 6 trillion, and contain 22 digits!!!

Web Help

Check out www.badastronomy. com (Phil Plait is the name of the person behind the site) for some background information for both you and your students. His video podcasts are interesting.

Book Tie-ins

What's Faster Than a Speeding Cheetah? by Robert E. Wells

Eyewitness: Light by David Burnie

Special Interests

The projects in this book dealing with astronauts and space were contributed by Joe Lennox.

In the early stages of this book, my sister Mary suggested that I contact Joe, a friend and work colleague of hers in the banking industry. Joe became interested in the space program when he was nine years old, and began collecting everything he could find related to the history-making missions of the time. His collection has grown into a space history museum, and he is active in teaching, consulting and writing.

Joe's memoir of how his life has been intertwined with the space program is called *Vision for Space*. He has also written a book for kids called *The ABCs of Space Exploration*, which is packed with easy-to-understand information. Here's an inspiration for kids with a big interest. Keep at it — you never know where it will lead!

Group Projects

These projects are great for group work. With a few whole-class lessons on cooperative learning strategies and accountability in groups, your students will achieve success both academically and socially.

Book Tie-ins

Beyond Monet: The Artful Science of Instructional Integration by Barrie Bennett and Carol Rolheiser

Classroom Management: A Thinking and Caring Approach by Barrie Bennett and Peter Smilanich

Choral Reading
Desert Island Adventure
Extra Fun Day
Flat Stanley
Hailstones and Halibut Bones
Math Olympics
Monthly Newsletter Written by the Class
Planet Walk
Play Money Spelling Bee
Precise Communication
Pumpkin Study
Reading Survey
Rock Review
School Multicultural Project
Shoes
Sugar Cube Creations
Think Outside the Box
Trivia Game Culminating Activity
Understanding Craters

Stop, Drop and Read Day

This can be as big as a whole school literacy event or as small as a single-class celebration of reading.

Grades K–8

Subjects Language Arts

Time Frame Any time period up to a full day

Materials Lots of reading materials

This can be a whole school literacy event. Some planning by a committee or the whole staff will make this special day run smoothly. It can run for any time period, depending on how you choose to organize it. Other possibilities are a single class, grade level or division celebration of reading. A solid structure will ensure a successful event. Make a schedule for the events so you can organize appropriate time frames for each type of reading.

Ideas:
- Everyone reads from individual books quietly for one minute, mark starting and finishing points, count the words read in one minute, and come up with a total number of words for each individual and for the class as a whole (Math tie-in).
- Everyone reads the same paragraph at the same time. Use a text that each student has, perhaps a page in a textbook or a photocopied page.
- Using a text that each student has, have a student read one word, then go around the whole class with each student reading one word.
- Lip reading: guess what the person is saying as they read without vocalizing.
- Share a book with a friend or group.
- Use atlases to look up place names. For example, find a place that has a girl's name, boy's name, name of a color, etc.
- Teacher reads to students.
- Choral reading: prepare a selection that you can present to another class (see page 36).
- Bring in some newspapers to share.
- Use a class set of dictionaries for "dictionary races" where students race to be the first to look up a word and read its meaning.
- Everyone reads aloud (different things) at the same time for one minute. This is silly and loud, but fun.

- Get a selection of picture books for students to read.
- Sing the words being read to the tune of the ABC song.
- Join up with a buddy class, so older students can read to younger ones, and younger ones can use a book to tell a story to older ones.
- Invite special guest readers (parents, the mayor, the principal, etc.) to the school to read to students or perhaps to read and discuss their favorite childhood book.
- Listen to an audio book (or part of one) together.

Book Tie-ins

Book! Book! Book!
by Deborah Bruss

- Have a collection of materials written in other languages and students can have fun trying to figure out how to pronounce the foreign words and their meanings.
- Organize your event so that students travel from one place to another for various types of reading. For example, one class could be designated for reading newspapers, one for magazines, one for atlas work, thus reducing the amount of materials each individual teacher must collect.
- Schedule a school-wide pizza lunch, charge the students a dollar a slice and donate the profits to the school library or a local food bank. Parent volunteers could organize this.
- Arrange an author visit as the highlight of the day.
- Design a certificate or bookmark that can be given to students at the end of the day.

Student Books Modeled on a Published Book

Use a book studied by your class as a model for student made books following the same pattern.

Grades K–8

Subjects Language Arts, possible tie-ins with Science, Social Studies, Math

Time Frame Several lessons

Materials A book to use as a pattern, paper and writing materials

Suggested texts to use as patterns:
Alexander and the Terrible, Horrible, No Good, Very Bad Day by Judith Viorst
A My Name is Alice by Jane Bayer (don't read the whole book first for this one, just study the "A" page)
What Do You Do? by Mercer Mayer

Children are great at following patterns. Choose a book to use as a pattern for the students to base their story on, and study its structure, pattern and sound using Shared Reading techniques. Model student books on the book the class has shared. Provide guidelines for your students as to the number of pages they should write.

Students could work on their own or with a partner or small group. Students should follow the usual writing process: write a rough copy first, edit first with peers then with teacher, then do a good copy with illustrations.

For younger students, the class could work together to create a book using shared writing techniques. *For middle and upper grade students,* provide as much structure as you think they require.

A girl named Arlene wrote a book called *Mrs. Mayne and the Terrible, Horrible, No Good, Very Bad Day* when she was in Grade 5, and gave me the book. (I was her teacher.) Arlene contacted me more than 20 years later when she became a teacher in my school board. We had a happy reunion when I met with her and returned the book to her. These are the kinds of moments you may be building when you give your students fun and memorable projects!

Web Help

Useful sites for directions on how to make books are:
www.makingbooks.com/freeprojects.shtml
www.vickiblackwell.com/makingbooks.html

Sugar Cube Creations

Possibilities are endless when children are challenged to build using sugar cubes.

Grades K–8

Subjects Social Studies, Art, Math

Time Frame Several introductory lessons, a couple of lessons to build the castle, one or two follow-up lessons

Materials Sugar cubes, something to stick cubes together (icing sugar and water mixed to make a paste, glue or another kind of icing), a base for building (square of cardboard covered in foil paper or a strong white foam plate, large or small depending on the project)

Cover a square piece of cardboard with foil paper. Build a structure using sugar cubes held together by one of the means above. Older students can be challenged to build without glue, relying on balance to hold the cubes together.

Ideas include:
* pyramid (6 cube by 6 cube base, then 5 by 5, 4 by 4, etc.)
* medieval castle (15 cube by 15 cube base works well)
* robot
* winter scene (build houses, glue cotton onto the base for snow, leave some foil showing for a skating rink)
* igloo
* a competition to see which group can build the tallest tower (*Guinness Book of World Records* lists the record-setting tower at 64 inches.)
* give students free rein to use their imaginations

Although the temptation is huge, students should be warned about eating sugar cubes as there have been occurrences of overindulgence and resultant illness!

Book Tie-ins

Cane to Sugar by Julie Murray
Sugar (True Books: Food and Nutrition) by Elaine Landau

Tap Dancing with Bottle Caps on Shoes

For a lively Daily Physical Activity or Phys. Ed. Session, have kids tap dance with bottle caps on the bottoms of their shoes.

Grades K–8

Subjects Phys. Ed.

Time Frame One lesson, repeat as desired

Materials Two metal bottle caps for the bottom of each student's shoe, masking tape

Have children tape a bottle cap smooth side down onto the bottom of each shoe. Use masking tape in an X shape; the bottle cap will still tap with the tape on top of it. Then teach some simple tap dancing moves. Fun!

If you have a parent or a student in the school who knows tap dancing, have them come in as a special guest instructor! If you're on your own, this website will teach you basic tap moves: www.ehow.com/how_18075_learn-basic-tap.html.

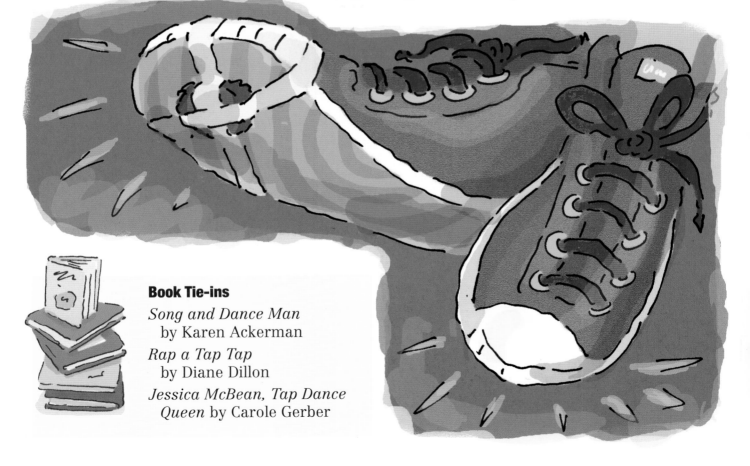

Book Tie-ins

Song and Dance Man by Karen Ackerman

Rap a Tap Tap by Diane Dillon

Jessica McBean, Tap Dance Queen by Carole Gerber

Ten Apples Up On Top

You can always count on Dr. Seuss for a fun time!

Grades K–2

Subjects Math, Art

Time Frame One or two lessons

Materials 12-by-18-inch white or cream paper for background; photocopied strips of paper with 10 apples on each strip (each apple about the size of a quarter, and set inside a box to make it easier for little hands to cut them out), coloring materials, scissors, glue

Read students the book *Ten Apples Up On Top* by Theo LeSieg. Discuss the book.

Teacher preparation: Use a piece of 12-by-18-inch white or cream colored paper for the activity. Turn the paper vertically. Leaving a little space at the top of the paper for the title, place 10 apples in a vertical row down the paper. At the spot where the last apple ends, fold the paper.

Students will draw and color a picture of themselves starting at the fold down to the bottom of the paper. Put the paper aside. Give students a strip of 10 apples. They will write the numbers 1 to 10 in the apples and color them red, green or yellow (tell them not to color over the numbers).

Then they will cut out the number 1 apple and glue it into position on the top of the head they drew, as on the cover of the book. Follow with apples 2 to 10, placing each

apple directly above the one below. Make sure they cut the apples out one at a time or you will have apples everywhere!

When they are finished cutting, they can add details to the picture: a sun, clouds, trees, and so on. Students who are more advanced could color the apples two or three different colors and arrange them in a pattern. Print the title 10 Apples Up On Top in the space at the top of the page. Some Kindergarten students may need the teacher to print the title.

Book Tie-ins

Ten Apples Up On Top by Theo LeSieg*

The Apple Pie Tree by Zoe Hall

How to Make an Apple Pie and See the World by Marjorie Priceman

Up! Up! Up! It's Apple-Picking Time by Jody Fickes Shapiro

*Did you know that Theo LeSieg was a pseudonym for Theodore Geisel, Dr. Seuss? LeSieg is Geisel spelled backwards!

Things I Like/Don't Like About School

Students will make a two-sided circle illustrating on one side Things I Like About School and on the other side Things I Do Not Like About School.

Grades 1–8

Subjects Art, Math

Time Frame One to two art lessons

Materials White Bristol board or heavy white paper, rulers and compasses for measuring, coloring materials

Start the students thinking about their favorite things about school as well as those they don't like as much.

Depending on grade level, students can measure with a compass, draw and cut out two circles from white paper or Bristol board (8 inch/20 cm diameter). Trace a circle about the size of a poker chip in the middle, and divide the rest into six sections.

Or trace a circle template and cut out two circles. Trace a circle about the size of a poker chip in the middle and divide the rest into six sections each.

Or use two precut circles divided into six sections.

In the middle circles, print the titles Things I Like About School on one side and Things I Do Not Like About School on the other. On the appropriate side, students draw and color six things they like about school, and six things they do not like about school. When they are finished, attach a piece of fishing wire and hang the wheels from the ceiling or from a bulletin board.

Book Tie-ins

I Love School
  by Philimon Sturges
Things I Like
  by Anthony Browne

Think Outside the Box

It's an expression often used in education, but this time it's literal!

Grades 3–8

Subjects Any

Time Frame A couple of lessons to introduce the project and go over requirements, a week or more for the work to be completed and mounted on the box, several days for presentations

Materials Large boxes (about the size of the cartons that photocopy paper comes in), white paper, construction paper

This project challenges students to display information and visuals on the outside of a large box, and to use the inside in a creative way connected to the topic.

Divide the students into groups. Each group will prepare a display on some aspect of the curriculum unit you choose to use for this project.

Examples:

Simple Machines: Each group would prepare the outside of their box with information

and illustrations that explain how their simple machine works, what it is useful for, definitions for specific

Web Help

Students may be interested in the "Nine Dot Puzzle," a classic puzzle whose solution lies in "thinking outside the box": www.dcu.ie/ctyi/puzzles/general/9dotpuz.htm

vocabulary related to their machine, photos or drawings showing examples of their simple machine. Perhaps a student-built model of their simple machine would be inside the box, or an experiment related to their simple machine that other students could try.

Transportation: Each group would work on a different mode of transportation such as car, airplane and boat. The outside of the box could contain a glossary of terms, famous examples, a labeled diagram of parts and photos or drawings. Inside the box could be a student-built model, a game based on the topic or other ideas as thought of by students.

Teacher expectations, of course, will be more complex at higher grade levels.

Book Tie-ins

Not a Box by Antoinette Portis
The Art Box by Gail Gibbons

Trading Card

Students will create a trading card in the style of sports team cards.

Grades 4–8

Subjects Art, Math

Time Frame Two or more Art lessons

Materials Bristol board or heavy white paper, coloring materials, rulers, scissors

Trading cards, especially for sports, have been popular with children for years. Many children's sports teams now provide their players with an individualized card carrying a photo and statistics.

Tell the students about the phenomenon of sports card collecting. Nowadays there are full sets that can be purchased intact, but in years gone by a person had to build a collection one card at a time. People take very good care of their cards now, storing them in plastic sleeves and keeping them in good condition, but years ago people played games with the cards, and played "for keeps."

You can also share card trivia with your students: trading cards first made their appearance in the late 1800s, they often accompanied the purchase of chewing gum or candy, and in 1991, a 1910 Honus Wagner baseball card was bought by Wayne Gretzky and his former boss for $451,000.

The subject of the trading card made by the students will be a real person, either themselves or a parent, hero or friend. Study several trading cards as a class, noting what type of information they contain. Discuss the need to be brief and concise in the written information. A little research may be needed to gather the information, either by an interview or in biographical material.

Web Help

An alternative assignment could be to create a trading card based on a fictional character from a novel study. The online card creator at http://www.readwritethink.org/materials/trading_cards/ can be used to create a card for a literary character.

Whole-School Projects

It's great when the whole school gets involved to produce a special day or special project. With some advance planning by the staff, these projects create a whole school buzz.

Extra Fun Day
Flat Stanley
Leaf Pictures
Monthly Newsletter Written By Students
Reading Awards
Reading Time
Read Posters
Report To Mission Control
School Multicultural Project
Stop, Drop and Read
Student Books Modeled On A Published Book
Sugar Cube Creations
Tap Dancing With Bottle Caps On Shoes
Things I Like/Don't Like About School
Trivia Quiz
Walkathon

After doing a rough copy, students will measure and cut out the card, then draw the picture on one side and print the information on the other. Traditional cards are 2.5 by 3.5 inches (approximately 6 x 9 cm). Give students a chance to present their cards to the class when finished, and then display them in plastic sleeves designed for trading cards.

Book Tie-ins

The Hockey Card by Jack Siemiatycki
Collecting Baseball Cards by Thomas S. Owens
Made In the USA – Trading Cards by Ryan A. Smith and Gary Tolle

Trivia Game Culminating Activity

A fun and different way to do a culminating activity is to have the students work in groups to organize a game show-like presentation in an assigned curriculum area.

Grades 4–8

Subjects Any

Time Frame One or two lessons to discuss format and expectations, several lessons for students to gather information and organize it into game form, several lessons for presentation/playing of the games

Materials Research material on the subject area you have chosen, paper, recipe cards, Bristol board, etc., for game construction

The class is divided into five groups. Each group is assigned a portion of the just-completed unit and is challenged to create a game based on a well-known trivia game using their research and or class notes. Games to be modeled can include Trivial Pursuit, Jeopardy, Twenty Questions, Who Wants to Be a Millionaire, Wheel of Fortune and Are You Smarter Than a Fifth Grader.

For example, a class studying Human Body Systems could divide into groups for digestive system (Trivial Pursuit), circulatory system (20 Questions), skeletal system (Jeopardy), and so on.

This project can also work for a novel study, history or geography unit.

To simplify the project for *middle grade students,* each group could create questions for the same game.

Trivia Quiz

This is not a review or test of curriculum, but general knowledge questions designed so that students learn at least one new piece of information each quiz. If they are getting all the answers right, the questions are too easy.

Grades K–8

Subjects All

Time Frame 5 to 10 minutes each time (as a special feature of a day or done weekly or at random intervals)

Materials 10 questions written by the teacher

A quiz can be written up very quickly by the teacher. Think about various school subjects as well as general knowledge of the world. If you keep your quiz questions in a notebook or binder, you can use them from year to year with a few adjustments for current events.

Students can jot the numbers 1 to 10 on a scrap piece of paper or in a notebook and write one-word answers. The quiz is taken up orally, and no record of marks is kept. In the days after the quiz, reference the answers to the most recent quiz to keep the information fresh in the students' minds.

Vary the level of difficulty and content according to grade. Be sure the questions are not too difficult. The average child should be able to score 5 to 7 on an average quiz. That way they will not be bombarded with new information and will not be frustrated by not being able to answer a single question.

Sample questions
(approximate level, Grades 4–6)

Name a state in the United States that begins with the letter A.

Name one thing you can find out about a word in a dictionary besides how to spell it.

Name a string instrument other than a guitar.

Who was the first human to walk on the moon?

Who is the mayor of our city?

A giraffe can clean its ears with its tongue: True or False?

Name one of the Great Lakes.

In which sport would you find a score called "love"?

What branch of science studies the planets?

Name a book by Dr. Seuss.

Book Tie-ins

If you have a reference section in your class library, students may be inspired to flip through the books in search of their own trivia questions and answers. This introduces them to and gives them familiarity with nonfiction information books.

Time for Kids: Almanac 2009
   by the editors of *Time for Kids* magazine

Tough Trivia for Kids by Helene Hovanec

Scholastic Book of Lists

World Almanac for Kids 2008 by the editors of the
   World Almanac for Kids and C. Alan Joyce

Understanding Craters

Most students know that the Moon has craters on its surface. They will be interested to learn that studying the craters gives scientists information about the geologic history of the Moon. This activity helps students to understand how the Moon craters were formed when meteorites, comets or asteroids crashed into the surface.

Grades 3–8

Subjects Science, Math, Art

Time Frame Two to three lessons

Materials Baking pan (9-by-13-inch size works well), flour, bread crumbs, a marble, a golf ball, a tennis ball, ruler, plastic sheet or newspaper to put under the pan to keep test area clean

Talk with students about craters and determine what they already know. Discuss their theories about how craters were formed.

Prepare one or more baking pans with a layer of breadcrumbs at least halfway up the pan. Cover with a layer of flour sifted on to the top. Add another thin layer of breadcrumbs on the top.

Drop one of the weights onto the pan one at a time. After each drop, measure the depth and width of the crater and observe the changes in the surface. Vary the height and angle at which weights are dropped. The spray of breadcrumbs and flour will approximate the way in which the inside surfaces of the

Moon are spread when impacted. It also illustrates that the materials buried deeper are geologically older, and are brought to the surface by the impacting objects.

Depending on the grade level and class size, this may be done as a whole-class activity, a teacher-directed demonstration, or student based in small groups.

Book Tie-ins

Discovering Crater Lake by Nancy Field

What the Moon is Like (Let's Read and Find Out Series) by Franklyn M. Branley

The Moon by Seymour Simon

Results may be tallied on a class chart, or individual student recording sheets. Grade level will determine the complexity of expectations for student responses. For example, *upper grade students* can write up the activity in experiment form, can compare the size and features of the craters, and can study the differences in craters formed by different sized weights. *Younger students* can write a journal entry describing the process and draw a picture.

This activity lends itself well to cooperative learning strategies. Students can be assigned roles in preparing, dropping the weights, recording, resurfacing the pan, and so on.

Extensions to this project can include finding out about and looking at pictures of famous craters on Earth such as those in Sudbury, Ontario, at Meteor Crater, Arizona, and at Wolfe Creek, Australia. Further exploration can be done into asteroids, meteorites and comets.

Walkathon

Involve the whole school in a fundraising walkathon. You can walk for charity, as a fundraiser for the school or for a special cause.

Grades K–8

Subjects Phys. Ed, Language Arts

Time Frame Organization and preparation time several months before the event, several hours for the event itself

Materials Materials provided by charitable organization, writing and art supplies, walkie-talkies for safety during the walk

A walkathon is a great way to build school spirit while raising funds. Get your school involved in an existing event or create your own. Form a team of staff members to organize the event several months in advance. Decide on a cause, plan out a route, arrange for fundraising and permission forms to be sent home to parents, organize an assembly to inform and motivate students (groups of students could write and perform skits or songs as a part of this), and arrange for parent volunteers to help with supervision.

There are many worthy causes to support, including autism awareness and research, cancer research, other societies that support those with a disease or condition (perhaps a student or family member in your school makes one of these causes close to your heart), local community initiatives or food banks, or your own school (library, playground equipment, or enhancing school programs).

Be sure to learn and follow the policies and protocols of your school district.

In the time leading up to the event, students can make posters, create jingles or slogans, do research or learn as a class about the cause you are supporting, and

read books on related subjects.

On the day of your walkathon, older students can team up with younger ones for safety and supervision. Many charitable organizations give out certificates, bookmarks or other awards to those participating in the event. Some will send a speaker to your school before the event.

After the event, students can write journal entries about their experience, contribute articles to the classroom or school newsletter, the school website and the local newspaper. Students can create murals and banners, make graphs to display the money earned by grade level, calculate the distance walked by one student then multiply to discover the total distance covered one class, one grade level or the whole school.

In Canada there is a National School Run Day to honor Terry Fox, a young man who lost his right leg to cancer at age 18. Terry was inspired to help other cancer patients. He decided to run across Canada to raise money for cancer research. Terry called his run the Marathon of Hope and he began on April 12, 1980, in St. John's, Newfoundland.

Book Tie-ins

Terry Fox: A Story of Hope
by Maxine Trottier
The Giving Book by Ellen Sabin
Somewhere Today:
A Book of Peace
by Shelley Moore Thomas

He asked each Canadian to contribute one dollar. After running 3,339 miles in 143 days, Terry was forced to stop running on September 1, 1980, in Thunder Bay, Ontario, as the cancer had returned and was in his lungs. Terry Fox died on June 28, 1981. The First Terry Fox Run was held in 1981 and 300,000 people participated. Today the Terry Fox Run involves millions of people in over 29 countries, and more than $400 million dollars has been raised. Each September school children celebrate Terry and the Marathon of Hope by walking or running with their schoolmates.

Start something that your school can look forward to annually for years to come.

Winter Garden

Bring some new life into your classroom!

Grades K–6

Subjects Science, Language Arts, Art, Math

Time Frame Several weeks

Materials Shallow dishes, water, sweet potato tops (approximately 1 inch), carrot tops (approximately ½ inch), fresh ginger, pineapple top with the green leaves in the center, garlic

This is a good project for the winter when colors outside are drab. Students enjoy seeing the changes and growth in the plants from day to day. The plants will not grow another fruit or vegetable, but will sprout and grow into bushy plants.

When choosing carrot tops, they should be approximately ½ inch long, including some orange and some green; a carrot that shows signs of a shoot on top will work best.

Place flat stones in a shallow dish, fill with water almost to the top of the dish, place carrot tops, sweet potato tops, ginger, etc., between or gently resting on top of the pebbles, but touching the water. Top up the water as required.

Observe the changes and growth that occurs. Chart the changes in Science notebooks (journal style), or on large chart paper (depending on grade level) both in writing and in diagrams. A digital photo journal could also be made.

In a manner appropriate for the grade level, have students write up observations.

Middle grade students could research further information about each fruit or vegetable including origins, vitamins and nutrients in each food, necessary growing conditions, etc. This could be done in groups, one for each type of vegetable you are growing.

Book Tie-ins

Grow It Again by Elizabeth MacLeod and Caroline Price

Growing Vegetable Soup by Lois Ehlert

Planting a Rainbow by Lois Ehlert

Word Art

In this activity, instead of coloring in shapes or shading them, students will print and repeat words related to the picture to fill in the area.

Grades 3–8

Subjects Art

Time Frame Two to three Art lessons

Materials Paper, coloring materials

Draw a picture (outline only) of a cartoon character, still life scene, person or any idea the student has. Fill in the open area with printed words related to the object or letters of the alphabet.

See the example here.

Be sure your students print in medium to large letters/words inside the outlines, or the project will take too long. *Middle grade students* should stick to two or three shapes on a page.

Bibliography

Ackerman, Karen. *Song and Dance Man*. New York: Knopf, 1988.

Adoff, Arnold. *Black Is Brown Is Tan*. New York: Amistad, 2004.

Agee, Jon. *The Incredible Painting of Felix Clousseau*. New York: Farrar, Straus and Giroux, 1990.

Alda, Arlene. *Arlene Alda's ABC*. Berkeley, California, Tricycle Press, 1993.

Allen, Judy. *Are You a Butterfly?* Boston: Kingfisher, 2003.

Allen, Judy. *Are You a Snail?* Boston: Kingfisher, 2003.

Allison, Catherine. *Brown Paper Bear*. New York: Scholastic, 2004.

Andersen, Hans Christian. *The Emperor's New Clothes*. Boston: Houghton Mifflin, 2004.

Ardley, Neil. *The Science Book of Color*. New York: Random House Value, 1995.

Armstrong, Thomas. *7 Kinds of Smart*. New York: Plume, 1999.

Armstrong, Thomas. *You're Smarter Than You Think: A Kid's Guide to Multiple Intelligences*. Minneapolis: Free Spirit, 2002.

Aronson, Steven M. L. *Trees: Trees Identified by Leaf, Bark & Seed*. New York: Workman, 1997.

Asch, Frank. *Mr. Maxwell's Mouse*. Toronto, New York: Kids Can Press, Ltd., 2004.

Atwell, Nancie. *In the Middle: New Understandings About Writing, Reading and Learning*. Portsmouth, NH: Boynton/Cook Publishers, 1998.

Atwell, Nancie. *The Reading Zone: How to Help Kids Become Skilled, Passionate, Habitual, Critical Readers*. New York: Scholastic Teaching Resources, 2007.

Badt, Karin Luisa. *On Your Feet (A World of Difference)*. Chicago: Children's Press, 1995.

Barker, Cicely Mary. *Flower Fairies Alphabet*. New York: Warne, 2009.

Bayer, Jane E. *A, My Name Is Alice*. New York: Puffin, 1992.

Baylor, Byrd. *Everybody Needs a Rock*. New York: Aladdin, 1985.

Baylor, Byrd. *The Way to Start a Day*. New York: Aladdin Books, 1986.

Beatrice, Paul. *Nifty Plates from the Fifty States: Take a Ride Across Our Great Nation: Learn About the States from Their License Plates!* New York: Applesauce Press, 2007.

Bennett, Barrie, and Carol Rolheiser. *Beyond Monet: The Artful Science of Instructional Integration*. London: Barrie Bennett, 2001.

Bennett, Barrie, and Peter Smilanich. *Classroom Management: A Thinking and Caring Approach*. Toronto: Bookation Inc., 1994.

Berenstain, Mike. *The Berenstain Bears and the Big Spelling Bee*. New York: HarperFestival, 2007.

Bianchi, John. *Young Author's Day at Pokeweed Public School*. Pokeweed Press, 2001.

Bird, E. J. *How Do Bears Sleep?* New York: Carolrhoda Books, 1990.

Bjork, Christina. *Linnea in Monet's Garden.* Stockholm: R. & S. Books, 1987.

Booth, David. *Even Hockey Players Read: Boys, Literacy and Reading.* Markham, Ontario: Pembroke Publishers, 2002.

Boraas, Tracey. *TV Reporters (Community Helpers).* New York: Capstone Press, 1999.

Boursin, Didier. *Folding for Fun: Origami for Ages 4 and Up.* New York: Firefly Books, 2007.

Boynton, Sandra. *Blue Hat, Green Hat.* New York: Little Simon, 1984.

Branley, Franklyn M., and True Kelley. *What the Moon Is Like.* New York: Harper Collins, 2000.

Brewster, Hugh. *At Vimy Ridge: Canada's Greatest World War I Victory.* Toronto: Scholastic Canada, 2006.

Brighton, Catherine. *Five Secrets in a Box.* New York: Dutton, 1987.

Bronson, Tammy Carter. *Tiny Snail.* Farmington, AK: Bookaroos Publishing Inc, 2002.

Brooks, Sue. *Fun with Butterflies Stencils (Dover Little Activity Books).* Minneapolis: Dover Publications, 1997.

Brown, Jeff. *Flat Stanley.* New York: HarperTrophy, 2003.

Brown, Marc. *D.W. the Picky Eater.* Boston: Little, Brown Young Readers, 1997.

Brown, Marcia. *Stone Soup: An Old Tale.* New York: Aladdin Books, 1986.

Browne, Anthony. *Things I Like.* New York: Knopf, 1989.

Bruss, Deborah. *Book! Book! Book!* New York: Arthur A. Levine Books, 2001.

Buckley, James Jr., and Robert Stremme. *Scholastic Book of Lists.* New York: Scholastic Reference, 2006.

Bull, John L. *National Audubon Society Field Guide to North American Birds.* New York: Knopf, 1994.

Burke, Judy. *Look What You Can Make With Paper Bags.* New York: Boyd's Mills Press, 1999.

Burnie, David. *Bird (DK Eyewitness Books).* New York: DK Children, 2008.

Burnie, David. *Eyewitness Light.* New York: DK Children, 1999.

Burningham, John. *Would You Rather....* New York: Sea Star Books, 1978.

Calkins, Lucy McCormick. *The Art of Teaching Reading.* New York: Longman, 2001.

Calkins, Lucy McCormick. *The Art of Teaching Writing.* Portsmouth, NH: Heinemann, 1994.

Calmenson, Stephanie. *The Principal's New Clothes.* New York: Atlantic, 1989.

Carle, Eric. *Little Cloud.* New York: Putnam Juvenile, 2001.

Carle, Eric. *Today Is Monday.* New York: Putnam Juvenile, 1997.

Carle, Eric. *The Very Hungry Caterpillar.* New York: Philomel Books, 1979.

Carter, David A. *One Red Dot: A Pop-Up Book for Children of All Ages.* New York: Little Simon, 2005.

Charney, Steve, and David Goldbeck. *The ABCs of Fruits and Vegetables and Beyond.* New York: Ceres Press, 2007.

Ching Hai, The Supreme Master. *The Birds in My Life.* Grand Rapids: The Supreme Master Ching Hai Intl. Assoc. Co., Ltd., 2007.

Christian, Peggy. *If You Find a Rock.* New York: Harcourt Inc, 2008.

Clements, Andrew. *The Report Card.* New York: Aladdin Books, 2005.

Cowhey, Dennis R. *What Does That Mean? The Personal Stories Behind Vanity License Plates*. Arlington Heights IL: Key Answer Products, 1994.

Cressy, Judith. *What Can You Do With a Paper Bag?* San Francisco: Chronicle Books in association with the Metropolitan Museum of Art, 2001.

Curtis, Chara M. *Fun Is a Feeling*. Boston: Illumination Arts Company, 1998.

Day, Alexandra. *Carl's Christmas*. New York: Farrar Straus Giroux, 1990.

Day, Alexandra. *Good Dog, Carl*. New York: Aladdin Paperbacks, 1997.

Day, John. *The Book of Clouds*. New York: Sterling, 2005.

de Maupassant, Guy. Ill. Gary Kelley. *The Necklace*. Mankato MN: Creative Education, 1992.

de Regniers, Beatrice Schenk. *What Can You Do With a Shoe?* New York: Turtleback Books, 2001.

DePaola, Tomie. *The Cloud Book*. New York: Holiday House, 1984.

Dillon, Leo, and Diane Dillon. *Rap A Tap Tap, Here's Bojangles — Think of That!* New York: Scholastic Inc, 2003.

Dunn, Jon L., and Jonathan Alderfer. *National Geographic Field Guide to the Birds of North America*. Washington, D.C.: National Geographic, 2006.

Dunn, Sonja. *All Together Now: 200 of Sonja Dunn's Best Chants*. Markham ON: Pembroke Publishers, 1999.

Dunn, Sonja. *Crackers & Crumbs: Chants for Whole Language*. Portsmouth, NH: Heinemann, 1990.

Dussling, Jennifer. *Looking at Rocks*. New York: Grosset & Dunlap, 2001.

Eco, Umberto. *The Bomb and the General*. London: Secker & Warburg, 1989.

Eco, Umberto. *The Three Astronauts*. London: Secker & Warburg, 1989.

Editors of *Time for Kids* magazine. *Time for Kids Almanac 2009*. Alexandria: Time for Kids, 2008.

Ehlert, Lois. *Eating the Alphabet: Fruits and Vegetables From A to Z*. San Diego: Harcourt Brace Jovanovich, 1989.

Ehlert, Lois. *Growing Vegetable Soup*. New York: Voyager Books, 1990.

Ehlert, Lois. *Leaf Man*. Orlando, FL: Harcourt, 2005.

Ehlert, Lois. *Planting a Rainbow*. New York: Voyager Books, 1992.

Ehlert, Lois. *Red Leaf, Yellow Leaf*. San Diego: Harcourt Brace Jovanovich, 1991.

Elting, Mary and Michael Folsom. *Q is for Duck: An Alphabet Guessing Game*. New York: Clarion Books, 1980.

Englart, Mindi. *How Do I Become A...? TV Reporter*. New York: Blackbirch Press, 2003.

Feber, Jane. *Creative Book Reports: Fun Projects With Rubrics for Fiction and Nonfiction*. New York: Maupin House, 2004.

Feldgus, Eileen G., and Isabell Cardonick. *Kid Writing*. Chicago: Wright Group, 1999.

Fershleiser, Rachel, and Larry Smith. *Not Quite What I Was Planning: Six-Word Memoirs by Writers Famous and Obscure*. New York: Harper Perennial, 2008.

Field, Nancy. *Discovering Crater Lake*. Minneapolis: Dog-Eared Publications, 1989.

Fitz-Gibbon, Sally. *Two Shoes, Blue Shoes, New Shoes*. Toronto: Fitzhenry and Whiteside, 2005.

Fleming, Denise. *Time to Sleep*. New York: Henry Holt and Co., 2001.

Floyd, Ted. *Smithsonian Field Guide to the Birds of North America*. New York: Collins, 2008.

Forest, Heather. *Stone Soup*. Little Rock, AK: August House, 1998.

Fowler, Allan. *A Snail's Pace*. New York: Children's Press, 1999.

Fowler, Allan. *It's a Fruit, It's a Vegetable, It's a Pumpkin*. Chicago: Children's Press, 1996.

Fox, Mem. *Radical Reflections: Passionate Opinions on Teaching, Learning, and Living*. San Diego: Harcourt Brace & Co., 1993.

Fox, Mem. *Shoes From Grandpa*. New York: Scholastic, 1996.

Fox, Mem. *Whoever You Are (Reading Rainbow Book)*. New York: Voyager Books, 2006.

Fraser, Kathleen, Laura and Mary. *The 175 Best Camp Games: A Handbook for Leaders*. Erin, ON: Boston Mills Press, 2009.

Galdone, Paul. *Henny Penny*. New York: Clarion Books, 1984.

Ganeri, Anita. *DK First Atlas (DK First Reference Series)*. New York: DK Children, 2004.

Gardner, Howard. *Frames of Mind: The Theory of Multiple Intelligences*. New York: BasicBooks, 1993.

Gerber, Carole. *Jessica McBean, Tap Dance Queen*. Austin, TX: Blooming Tree Press, 2005.

Gerstein, Mordicai. *The Man Who Walked Between the Towers*. New York: Square Fish, 2007.

Gibbons, Gail. *Art Box*. New York: Sagebrush, 2000.

Giovanni, Nikki, ed. *Hip Hop Speaks to Children*. Naperville, IL: Sourcebooks Inc., 2008.

Gomi, Taro. *My Friends/Mis Amigos*. New York: Chronicle Books, 2006.

Granfield, Linda. *In Flanders Fields: The Story of the Poem by John McCrae*. Toronto: Fitzhenry and Whiteside, 1997.

Green, John. *Little Butterflies Stained Glass Coloring Book*. Mineola, NY: Dover Publications, 1992.

Grey, Mini. *The Very Smart Pea and the Princess-to-be*. New York: Alfred A. Knopf, 2003.

Guthrie, Woody. *Mail Myself to You (Let Me Read, Level 2)*. New York: GoodYear Books, 1994.

Hall, Margaret. *Hibernation (Patterns in Nature)*. New York: Capstone Press, 2006.

Hall, Zoe. *The Apple Pie Tree*. New York: Scholastic, 1996.

Hall, Zoe. *It's Pumpkin Time!* New York: Scholastic Paperbacks, 1999.

Hamanaka, Sheila. *All the Colors of the Earth* (Mulberry Books). New York: HarperTrophy, 1999.

Hannah, Julie, and Joan Holub. *The Man Who Named the Clouds*. Boston: Albert Whitman & Company, 2006.

Hargreaves, Roger. *Little Miss Fun* (Mr. Men and Little Miss). New York: Price Stern Sloan, 2001.

Harwayne, Shelley. *Lasting Impressions*. Portsmouth, NH: Heinemann, 1992.

Hayden, Kate. *DK Readers: Astronaut, Living in Space (Level 2: Beginning to Read Alone)*. New York: DK Children, 2000.

Hayward, Linda. *DK Readers: Jobs People Do — A Day in the Life of a TV Reporter*. New York: DK Children, 2001.

Heard, Georgia. *Awakening the Heart: Exploring Poetry in Elementary and Middle School*. Portsmouth, NH: Heinemann, 1999.

Heard, Georgia. *For the Good of the Earth and Sun: Teaching Poetry*. Portsmouth, NH: Heinemann, 1989.

Heidbreder, Robert, and Scot Ritchie. *Eenie Meenie Manitoba*. Toronto, New York: Kids Can Press, Ltd., 2000.

Heligman, Deborah. *From Caterpillar to Butterfly*. New York: Harper Collins, 1996.

Hepworth, Cathi. *Antics*. New York: G.P. Putnam's Sons, 1992.

Higgs, Liz Curtis. *The Sunflower Parable: Special 10th Anniversary Edition*. Nashville TN: Thomas Nelson, 2007.

Hoban, Tana. *So Many Circles, So Many Squares*. New York: Greenwillow Books, 1998.

Hooks, Bell. *Be Boy Buzz*. New York: Jump at the Sun, 2005.

Hooper, Meredith. *The Pebble in My Pocket*. New York: Frances Lincoln Children's Books, 1997.

Hovanec, Helene. *Tough Trivia for Kids (Mensa)*. New York: Sterling, 2005.

Hutchins, Pat. *Don't Forget the Bacon!* New York: Mulberry Books, 1994.

Innocenti, Roberto. *Rose Blanche*. Boston: Creative Company, 2003.

Jackson, Ellen B. *Cinder Edna*. New York: Lothrop, Lee & Shepard, 1994.

Jackson, Paul. *Folding Paper Fun*. London: Michael O'Mara Books, 2007.

Jam, Teddy. *The Kid Line*. Toronto: Douglas & McIntyre, 2001.

Joyce, C. Alan. *The World Almanac for Kids 2008*. Chicago: World Almanac, 2007.

Kelley, True. *Pablo Picasso: Breaking All the Rules (Smart About Art)*. New York: Grosset & Dunlap, 2002.

Kennedy, Paul E. *Fun With Leaves: Stencils (Dover Little Activity Book)*. Minneapolis: Dover Publications, 1991.

King, Elizabeth. *The Pumpkin Patch*. New York: Puffin Books, 1996.

Kloske, Geoffrey. *Once Upon a Time, The End: Asleep in 60 Seconds*. New York: Atheneum Books for Young Readers, 2005.

Korman, Gordon. *Escape (Island, Book 3)*. New York: Scholastic Inc., 2001.

Korman, Gordon. *Shipwreck (Island, Book 1)*. New York: Scholastic Paperbacks, 2001.

Korman, Gordon. *Survival (Island, Book 2)*. New York: Scholastic Inc., 2001.

Ladner, Cobi. *Why Is an Orange Called an Orange?* Boston: McArthur & Company, Ltd., 2003.

Landau, Elaine. *Sugar (True Books — Food & Nutrition)*. New York: Children's Press, 2000.

Lennox, Joe. *The ABCs of Space Exploration*. Centennial, CO: Life Vest, 2008.

Lennox, Joe. *Vision for Space: The Winding Journey Through Life and the Space Program as Seen by an Ordinary Joe*. Lincoln NE: IUniverse, Inc., 2004.

LeSieg, Theo. *Ten Apples Up On Top!* New York: Random House Books for Young Readers, 1961.

Lester, Alison. *Clive Eats Alligators*. Houghton Mifflin, 1991.

Lester, Alison. *When Frank Was Four*. Boston, MA: Houghton Mifflin Co., 1996.

Levenson, George. *Pumpkin Circle: The Story of a Garden*. New York: Tricycle Press, 2002.

Llewellyn, Claire. *Slugs and Snails (Minibeasts)*. New York: Franklin Watts, 2002.

Lobel, Anita. *Alison's Zinnia*. New York: Greenwillow Books, 1990.

Locker, Thomas. *Cloud Dance*. New York: Voyager Books, 2003.

MacLeod, Elizabeth. *Grow It Again (Kids Can Do It)*. Toronto, New York: Kids Can Press, Ltd., 1998.

Martel, Jane G. *Smashed Potatoes: A Kid's-eye View of the Kitchen*. Boston: Houghton Mifflin, 1974.

Marzollo, Jean. *I Am a Leaf*. New York: Scholastic, 1998.

Mayer, Mercer. *What Do You Do With a Kangaroo?* New York: Scholastic Inc., 1973.

McCallum, Ann. *The Secret Life of Math: Discover How (and Why) Numbers Have Survived From the Cave Dwellers to Us!* Nashville, TN: Williamson Books, 2005.

McNamara, Margaret. *Fall Leaf Project*. New York: Aladdin Paperbacks, 2006.

Menchin, Scott. *Taking a Bath With the Dog and Other Things That Make Me Happy*. Cambridge MA: Candlewick, 2007.

Menzel, Peter. *Material World: A Global Family Portrait*. San Francisco: Sierra Club Books, 1994.

Micklethwait, Lucy. *An Alphabet in Art (I Spy)*. London: HarperCollins Children's Books, 1992.

Milbourne, Anna. *How Big Is a Million? (Picture Books)*. New York: Usborne Books, 2008.

Miller, Millie. *Country-by-Country Guide (Our World)*. New York: Scholastic Reference, 2006.

Morris, Ann. *Shoes, Shoes, Shoes*. New York: Lothrop, Lee & Shepard Books, 1995.

Murray, Julie. *Cane to Sugar (Beginning to End)*. New York: Buddy Books, 2006.

Neitzel, Shirley. *The Jacket I Wear in the Snow*. New York: HarperTrophy, 1994.

Nolan, Dennis. *Dinosaur Dream*. New York: Aladdin Paperbacks, 1994.

O'Callahan, Jay. *Tulips*. Atlanta: Peachtree, 1996.

O'Connor, Jane. *Henri Matisse: Drawing with Scissors (Smart About Art)*. New York: Grosset & Dunlap, 2002.

O'Neill, Mary. *Hailstones and Halibut Bones*. New York: Doubleday Books for Young Readers, 1990.

Oppenheim, Joanne, and Barbara Reid. *Have You Seen Birds?* New York: Scholastic, 1990.

Owens, Thomas S. *Collecting Baseball Cards*. New York: Millbrook Press, 2000.

Pallotta, Jerry. *Flower Alphabet Book*. Watertown, MA: Charlesbridge Publishing, 1988.

Paschen, Elise, ed. *Poetry Speaks to Children*. Naperville IL: Sourcebook MediaFusion, 2005.

Pascoe, Elaine. *Scholastic Kid's Almanac: Facts, Figures, and Stats*. New York: Scholastic Reference, 2004.

Peddle, Daniel. *Snow Day*. New York: Doubleday Books for Young Readers, 2000.

Philpot, Graham. *Amazing Anthony Ant*. New York: Random House Books for Young Readers, 1994.

Pogue, William R. *How Do You Go to the Bathroom in Space?* New York: Tom Doherty Associates, 1999.

Portis, Antoinette. *Not a Box*. New York: HarperCollins, 2006.

Poydar, Nancy. *Bad News Report Card*. New York: Holiday House, 2006.

Preller, James. *Wake Me in Spring*. New York: Scholastic, 1994.

Prelutsky, Jack, comp. *The Random House Book of Poetry for Children*. New York: Random House Value, 1983.

Prelutsky, Jack. *My Dog May Be a Genius*. New York: Greenwillow, 2008.

Prelutsky, Jack. *The New Kid on the Block*. New York: Greenwillow Books, 1984.

Prevert, Jacques. *How to Paint the Portrait of a Bird*. New York: Roaring Brook Press, 2007.

Priceman, Marjorie. *How to Make an Apple Pie And See the World*. New York: Knopf, 1994.

Rappaport, Doreen. *Martin's Big Words: The Life of Dr. Martin Luther King, Jr.* New York: Jump at the Sun, 2007.

Raschka, Chris. *Yo! Yes?* New York: Scholastic Inc., 2007.

Rau, Dana Meachen. *Circles*. Tarrytown, N.Y: Marshall Cavendish Benchmark, 2006.

Rau, Dana Meachen. *Space Walks (Our Solar System)*. New York: Compass Point Books, 2004.

Ray, Rachael. *Cooking Rocks! Rachael Ray 30-Minute Meals for Kids*. New York: Lake Isle Press, 2004.

Reed, Jennifer. *Picture This! Graphic Organizers*. Poulsbo, WA: Barker Creek, 2007.

Richards, Jean. *A Fruit Is a Suitcase for Seeds*. Minneapolis: First Avenue Editions, 2006.

Richardson, Wendy. *Families: Through the Eyes of Artists (World of Art Series)*. Chicago: Children's Press, 1991.

Ringgold, Faith. *Aunt Harriet's Underground Railroad in the Sky*. New York: Dragonfly Books, 1995.

Rosen, Michael. *No Breathing in Class*. London: Puffin Books, 2002.

Rosen, Michael. *Poems for the Very Young*. Boston: Kingfisher, 2004.

Rosen, Michael. *When Did You Last Wash Your Feet?* London: Lions, 1987.

Rosenthal, Amy Krouse. *Cookies: Bite-Size Life Lessons*. New York: HarperCollins, 2006.

Routman, Regie. *Reading Essentials: The Specifics You Need to Teach Reading Well*. Portsmouth, NH: Heinemann, 2003.

Ryder, Joanne. *Snail's Spell*. New York: Puffin Books, 1988.

Ryder, Joanne. *Where Butterflies Grow*. New York: Puffin, 1996.

Rylant, Cynthia. *When I Was Young in the Mountains (Reading Rainbow Books)*. New York: Puffin, 1993.

Sabin, Ellen. *The Giving Book: Open the Door to a Lifetime of Giving*. New York: Watering Can Press, 2004.

Sabuda, Robert. *Cookie Count: A Tasty Pop-Up*. New York: Little Simon, 1997.

Schaefer, Lola M. *This Is the Sunflower*. New York: Greenwillow Books, 2000.

Schmid, Eleonore. *Outside-Inside: Sweet Sour Juicy*. London: Burke, 1985.

Schuett, Stacey. *Somewhere in the World Right Now*. Albuquerque, NM: Dragonfly Books, 1997.

Schuette, Sarah L. *Circles (A+ Books: Shapes)*. New York: Capstone Press, 2002.

Schwartz, David M. *How Much Is a Million?* New York, NY: Mulberry Books, 1993.

Scieszka, Jon. *Math Curse*. New York: Viking, 1995.

Scieszka, Jon. *Science Verse*. New York: Viking Juvenile, 2007.

Seuss, Dr. *Ten Apples Up On Top!* New York: Random House Books for Young Readers, 1961.

Shannon, George. *Tomorrow's Alphabet.* New York: Greenwillow Books, 1996.

Shapiro, Jody Fickes. *Up, Up, Up! It's Apple-Picking Time.* New York: Scholastic, 2004.

Shaw, Charles G. *It Looked Like Spilt Milk.* New York: HarperTrophy, 1988.

Siemiatycki, Jack, and Avi Slodovnick. *The Hockey Card.* New York: Lobster Press, 2004.

Silverstein, Shel. *Falling Up.* New York: HarperCollins, 1996.

Silverstein, Shel. *A Light in the Attic.* New York: Harper & Row, 1981.

Silverstein, Shel. *Where the Sidewalk Ends* New York: HarperCollins, 2004.

Simmonds, Posy. *Lulu and the Flying Babies.* New York: Knopf, 1988.

Simon, Seymour. *The Moon.* New York: Simon & Schuster Books for Young Readers, 2003.

Sis, Peter. *The Wall: Growing Up Behind the Iron Curtain.* New York: Farrar, Straus and Giroux, 2007.

Sis, Peter. *Tibet: Through the Red Box.* New York: Farrar Straus Giroux, 1998.

Smith, David J. *If the World Were a Village: A Book About the World's People.* Toronto: Kids Can Press, 2005.

Smith, Ryan A. *Made in the USA: Trading Cards.* New York: Blackbirch Press, 2005.

Sohi, Morteza E. *Look What I Did With a Leaf.* New York: Walker Books for Young Readers, 1995.

Soto, Gary. *Snapshots From the Wedding.* New York: Putnam Juvenile, 1998.

Staub, Frank. *The Kids' Book of Clouds & Sky.* New York: Sterling, 2005.

Steig, William. *Abel's Island.* New York: Square Fish, 2007.

Steig, William. *Pete's a Pizza.* North Mankato, MN: Live Oak Media, 2004.

Sturges, Philemon. *I Love School!* New York: Scholastic Inc., 2005.

Symes, R. F. *Rocks & Minerals (DK Eyewitness Books).* New York: DK Children, 2008.

Taback, Simms. *There Was an Old Lady Who Swallowed a Fly.* New York: Viking, 1997.

Taback, Simms. *This Is the House that Jack Built.* New York: Puffin, 2004.

Tang, Greg. *The Grapes of Math.* New York: Scholastic Paperbacks, 2004.

Thomas, Shelley Moore. *Somewhere Today: A Book of Peace.* Boston: Albert Whitman & Company, 2002.

Titherington, Jeanne. *Pumpkin, Pumpkin.* New York: HarperTrophy, 1990.

Trueit, Trudi Strain. *Clouds (Watts Library).* New York: Franklin Watts, 2002.

Trottier, Maxine. *Terry Fox: A Story of Hope.* Toronto: Scholastic Canada Ltd., 2005.

Tsuchiya, Yukio. *Faithful Elephants: A True Story of Animals, People, and War.* Boston: Houghton Mifflin, 1997.

Tunnell, Michael O. *Mailing May.* New York: HarperTrophy, 2000.

Turkle, Brinton. *Deep in the Forest.* New York: Puffin, 1992.

Van Allsburg, Chris. *The Mysteries of Harris Burdick.* Boston: Houghton Mifflin, 1984.

Van Allsburg, Chris. The *Wretched Stone.* Boston: Houghton Mifflin, 1991.

Van Allsburg, Chris. *Two Bad Ants.* Boston: Houghton Mifflin, 1988.

Venezia, Mike. *Monet (Getting to Know the World's Greatest Artists).* New York: Children's Press, 1990.

Venezia, Mike. *Van Gogh (Getting to Know the World's Greatest Artists)*. New York: Children's Press, 1989.

Viorst, Judith. *Alexander and the Terrible, Horrible, No Good, Very Bad Day*. New York: Aladdin Books, 1987.

Waber, Bernard. *Lyle, Lyle, Crocodile*. San Francisco: Trumpet Club, 1988.

Wallace, Ian. *Boy of the Deeps*. Toronto: Groundwood Books, 2005.

Wallace, Ian. *Mavis and Merna*. Toronto: Groundwood Books, 2005.

Wallace, Ian. *The Sleeping Porch*. Toronto: Groundwood Books, 2008.

Wallace, Karen. *A Bed for the Winter (DK Readers Level 1)*. New York: Dorling Kindersley, 2000.

Wallace, Karen. *Born to Be a Butterfly (DK Readers, Level 1: Beginning to Read)*. New York: DK Children, 2000.

Walton, Rick. *So Many Bunnies*. New York: Lothrop, Lee and Shepard Books, 1998.

Wargin, Kathy-Jo, and Gijsbert Van Frankenhuyzen. *The Edmund Fitzgerald: Song of the Bell Edition 1. (True Story)*. New York: Sleeping Bear Press, 2003.

Wells, Robert E. *What's Faster Than a Speeding Cheetah?* Morton Grove, IL: Albert Whitman and Company, 1997.

Wells, Ruth. *A to Zen*. New York: Simon and Shuster Books for Young Readers, 1992.

Westcott, Nadine Bernard. *Never Take a Pig to Lunch*. New York: Scholastic, 1994.

Whalley, Paul. *Eyewitness Butterfly & Moth (Eyewitness Books)*. New York: DK Children, 2000.

Wiesner, David. *Free Fall*. New York: HarperCollins, 2008.

Willard, Nancy. *Simple Pictures Are Best*. Scholastic Inc., 1994.

Williams, Karen Lynn. *Galimoto (Reading Rainbow Book)*. New York: HarperTrophy, 1991.

Wise, Leonard. *The Way Cool License Plate Book*. New York: Firefly Books, 2002.

Wynne-Jones, Tim. *Some of the Kinder Planets*. New York: Puffin, 1996.

Yolen, Jane. *All Those Secrets of the World*. Boston: Little Brown and Company, 1993.

Yolen, Jane. *Color Me a Rhyme: Nature Poems for Young People*. New York: Boyds Mills Press, 2003.

Zelver, Patricia. *The Wonderful Towers of Watts (Reading Rainbow Books)*. New York: Boyds Mills Press, 2005.

Ziefert, Harriet. *39 Uses for a Friend*. New York: Putnam's, 2001.

Zimmerman, W. Frederick. *The World Is Flat: Not! Cool New World Maps for Kids*. New York: Nimble Books, 2006.

Web Resources

American Library Association Store: www.alastore.ala.org

Bad Astronomy/Discover Magazine: www.badastronomy.com

Character Trading Cards: www.readwritethink.org/materials/trading_cards/

Creating Graphic Organizers With Word Techtorial: www.education-world.com/a_tech/techtorial/techtorial095.pdf

Effective Parent Teacher Communication: www.priceless-teaching-strategies.com/parent_teacher_communication.html

Epals: www.epals.com

GPN Educational Media: www.shopgpn.com

How to Learn Basic Tap Dance Steps: www.ehow.com search How to Learn Basic Tap Dance Steps

Improving Parent-Teacher Interviews: www.canadianliving.com/family/parenting/ask_an_expert_improving_parent_teacher_interviews.php

International Space Station: EVA: http://spaceflight.nasa.gov/station/eva/spacesuit.html

The Learning Carpet: www.thelearningcarpet.ca

License Plates of the World: www.worldlicenseplates.com/

Library Video: www.libraryvideo.com

Little Giraffes Teaching Ideas: www.littlegiraffes.com

Making Books With Children: www.makingbooks.com/freeprojects.shtml

Microcinema International DVD: www.microcinemadvd.com

Mrs. Jones' Room: www.mrsjonesroom.com

The Mysteries of Harris Burdick: www.themysteriesofharrisburdick.com

The Nine Dot Puzzle: www.dcu.ie/ctyi/puzzles/general/9dotpuz.htm

The Official Flat Stanley Project: www.flatstanleyproject.com

Six-Word Memoirs by Smith Magazine: www.smithmag.net/sixwords/

The Snail by Henri Matisse (Tate Gallery animated display): www.tate.org.uk/imap/pages/animated/cutout/matisse/snail.htm

So You Have to Do a Research Project: www.ri.net/schools/East_Greenwich/research.html#organizing

Sound Venture Productions: www.soundventure.com/onlinestore

Tech-It & Take-It — Making Books with Children: www.vickiblackwell.com/makingbooks.html

Technology for Teachers: www.wacona.com/technology/tech4teacher.html

Tips for Parent-Teacher Interviews in 12 Languages: www.peopleforeducation.com/parent-teacher

US Space Suits: www.hightechscience.org/us_space_suits.htm

Using Computers in the Primary School: www.schools.ash.org.au/revesby

Webquest: www.webquest.org

Thanks

Ideas for projects are everywhere. Bring your life into the classroom. Bring the world into your classroom. Be inspired by things you see, hear, read and experience. Make connections. Use your imagination. Borrow and share ideas. Have fun!

The projects in this book were contributed by teachers who have used and enjoyed them in their classrooms. Some are original, some are classic, and some have been borrowed, shared, recycled and refreshed, their origins long forgotten. The name beside each project denotes the person who contributed it to this collection.

Agenda Day: Betty Borowski

Alphabet Adventure: gathered from places A to Z

Amaryllis Plant: adapted from the annual Christmas gift of Sandra Valeriote to her aunts Bruna Gumieniak and Emma Hohenadel

Art Project: Betty Borowski

Birds: adapted from the interests of Grade 4/5 students 1984–1985, St. Jean Brebeuf School, Brampton, Ontario

Book Report in a Bag: contributed by a teacher who got the idea from a student's mother, who was also a teacher

Book Talk on Video: adapted from the TV show *Reading Rainbow*

Books for Younger Students: Dorothy Thurley

Brown Paper Characters: Dallas Borris

Butterfly Life Cycle in Pasta: Fatima Wittemund

Choral Reading: adapted from a school visit by Sonja Dunn

Circles: adapted from a presentation by an OISE professor, 1980–1981

Computer-Made Graphic Organizer: Darlene Halchuk

Create a Country: Dagmar Batz

Desert Island Adventure: Gay Baile

Earth Day Globes: Dallas Borris

Extra Fun Day: Mindy Inglese

Family Portrait: Betty Borowski

First Day of School Questionnaire: adapted from a conference presentation by Nancie Atwell

Flat Stanley: worldwide project begun in 1995 by Dale Hubert

Folded Paper Art: inspired by the "cootie catchers" popular in Grade 4 in the 1980s

Friendship Hearts: inspired by the camaraderie and care for each other of Kindergarten students 2003–2008, St. Francis of Assisi School, Mississauga, Ontario

Fruit or Vegetable Drawing: Betty Borowski

Graduated Page-Length Books: Lillian Wos

Group Share After Reading: adapted from a presentation by Nancie Atwell

Hailstones and Halibut Bones: adapted from the book by Mary O'Neill

Hear and Draw: Deb Conderan

Hibernation Day: Fatima Wittemund

It Looked Like Spilt Milk: inspired by the book of the same name by Charles G. Shaw

Leaf Pictures: Vic Ohinski

Leaf Project: Kilmna Vasquez

License Plates: Betty Borowski

Math Olympics: Deb Conderan

Monthly Newsletter Written By Students: a project done with the Grade 3 students of 1998, St. Francis of Assisi School,

Mississauga, Ontario during the 6 weeks I had the pleasure of team teaching in their class

Multiple Intelligences Booklet: adapted from Professional Development Institute presentation by Barrie Bennett

The Mysteries of Harris Burdick: inspired by the book by Chris Van Allsburg

Page One: adapted from a presentation by Nancie Atwell

Planet Walk: Joe Lennox, founder of the largest private museum of space memorabilia and artifacts in the United States and author of *Vision for Space* and *The ABC's of Space Exploration*

Play Dough Predictor: remembered from a Summer Institute course

Play Money Spelling Bee: remembered from the first teacher project book I ever purchased in the summer of 1981

Poetry Circle: inspired by the fabulous poetry units of Betty Borowski

Postcards: Betty Borowski

The Principal's New Clothes: adapted from an idea by Lillian Wos

Pumpkin Study: an investigation done by my very first class, Grade 6, 1981–1982

Reading Awards: Darlene Halchuk

Reading Survey: adapted from a presentation by Shelley Harwayne

Reading Time: developed for and with the Grade 4 students of 1995–1996, who loved their books and their reading time!

Read Posters: from the American Library Association (ALA) website

Report to Mission Control: Joe Lennox

Rock Review: adapted from a long-ago magazine article

School Multicultural Project: teachers of St. Christopher School, Mississauga, Ontario, 2007

Self-Evaluation: Betty Borowski

Shoes: inspired by the "back to school" shoes of the 1994–1995 Grade 4/5 class at St. Francis of Assisi School, Mississauga, Ontario

Simulated Space Walk: Joe Lennox

Six Word Memoirs: adapted from the book *Not Quite What I Was Planning: Six-Word Memoirs by Writers Famous and Obscure* by Larry Smith and Rachel Fershleiser

Smashed Potatoes: Betty Borowski

Snail Terrarium: Lillian Wos

Speed of Light: Joe Lennox

Stop Drop and Read: teachers of St. Francis of Assisi School, Mississauga, Ontario

Student Books Modeled on a Published Book: Lisa Marie Marasco, Laura Fraser

Sugar Cube Creations: Barb Butler

Tap Dancing With Bottle Caps on Shoes: Betty Borowski

Ten Apples Up On Top: inspired by the book by Theo LeSieg

Things I Like / Do Not Like About School: Betty Borowski

Think Outside the Box: Stephanie Smith-Abram

Trading Card: inspired by the interests of Grade 4 boys at St. Francis of Assisi School, Mississauga, Ontario, in the 1990s

Trivia Game Culminating Activity: Stephanie Smith-Abram

Trivia Quiz: originally seen in an intermediate classroom in one of my first schools.

Understanding Craters: Joe Lennox

Walkathon: inspired by the Terry Fox Run

Winter Garden: Kilmna Vasquez

Word Art: a classic

Grateful thanks to Kathy Penn, Mary Lou West, Kirk Lemon, Cynthia Davidson and Jo-Ann Saliba.

For their help with organizing the Contents and Index pages, thanks to the dynamic duo of Maddy Mayne and Erin Gumieniak.

Index

When seeking projects for this book, it took only a close-to-shore casting of the fishing net to reap more than enough material for one volume.

We invite you to submit your great teacher projects
for possible inclusion in a future book.

Please send your ideas, along with your name, location, and contact information to greatteacherprojects@gmail.com.